THE SEARCH FOR GENERAL MILES

The Search
for
General Miles

Newton F. Tolman

G. P. PUTNAM'S SONS
NEW YORK

Copyright © 1968 by Newton F. Tolman

Excerpts from *Fighting Years* by Oswald Garrison Villard
reprinted by permission of the publisher,
Harcourt, Brace & World, Inc.

Library of Congress Catalog
Card Number: 68-15612

"Half-way through the labour of an index to this book I recalled the practice of my ten years' study of history; and realized I had never used the index of a book fit to read. Who would insult his Decline and Fall, by consulting it just upon a specific point?"

T. E. LAWRENCE
Seven Pillars of Wisdom

THE SEARCH FOR GENERAL MILES

1

MAYBE it was because the old boy looked so much like Great-Uncle Frank Parker, our own family's legendary hero. The same rather fiercely direct gaze and sweeping white moustache and prominent square jaw. Anyway, from that day about eight years ago when I first saw him staring down at me from the big portrait on the wall, the mystery of this man has continued to haunt me.

Not that I felt, then, that the mystery would present any real problem. Gen. Nelson A. Miles was obviously the town's most famous native son, and the musty attic museum where I stood was filled with memorabilia of his exploits. Flags, uniforms, swords, Indian relics, no end of it, all with an aura of long-gathering dust. And downstairs, in the shelves of the village library, there would be encyclopedias and histories, and probably a biography or two.

I had just taken on the job of editing, which meant mostly writing, a town history for the Historical Society of the small country township of Westminster, Massachusetts. A casual glance around the jam-packed little museum hidden away above the library suggested something special—a separate essay, even—might be in order on the subject of the General.

But when I came to question some of the older inhabitants about Miles' specific role in military history, their answers seemed always to be strangely evasive. Everyone was quite

9

sure that someone else in town must know all about Miles, but I could never seem to find the right person. In which wars did he serve? Nobody was quite sure, though some thought he was most prominent in the Spanish-American affair. Exactly what rank had he held? Nobody was at all sure of that.

Even the widow of the General's nephew (he had been the last Miles relative to live in Westminster), though she'd heard a little more about the family background, had an impression of Miles' career as sketchy as that of a Harvard professor of American history I questioned a little later on. And *he* came up with no more than I remembered from my own school days—only that Miles had commanded some forces, somewhere, during the Spanish-American War.

Some months went by before I came to the point in my town history manuscript where the Miles story would best fit in. I'd been sweating through several bushels of handwritten notes on such exciting subjects as Town Cemeteries, Highways, Waterworks and Sewers; many little industries, too, together with an old streetcar line, all long gone and unmourned; and I was sorry their musty old records hadn't departed along with them. I had almost forgotten the General.

I decided to begin back at the library, a handsome 1902 brick and stone edifice typical of its time—neo-Gothic, squat, and somewhat gloomy, but so solidly built it will defy the ages unless some future superhighway needs the space.

When I asked the librarian, a pleasant little local lady of long tenure, if she had any biographies of Nelson A. Miles, she said she didn't think so. But she would see what she could find in her reference listings. After my long and diligent poring over the latter, it began to look as though no biography of Miles had ever been published.

I remember thinking, at the time, there was something quite odd about this.

In the file the Historical Society had given me on Miles, there was little besides the genealogical stuff except a stack of obits clipped from newspapers when he died. Back in my cozy corner of the oak-paneled reading room, I went over the clippings. The most detailed was an AP dispatch from Washington, D.C., May 15, 1925. It began: "Lieut. Gen. Nelson A. Miles, nestor of American Army leaders, premier Indian Fighter, diplomat and author, has taken up the Long Trail. . . ."

Among the long-winded and flowery tributes, certain lines stood out as possible quotes for my working notes. ". . . one of the most distinguished and picturesque leaders in American military history . . . was one of the 'boy generals' of the Civil War. At the age of 25 he had risen from the rank of 1st Lieutenant of volunteers to that of Major General, and was commanding an entire army division of 25,000 men . . . at the peak of his career was commanding General of the Army, was one of the few high-ranking officers of the regular establishment to attain his position without West Point training. . . ."

Well, we were getting somewhere. Even though the obituaries raised almost as many questions about the man, in my mind at least, as they answered. But the accounts of the funeral were quite complete. It was an affair of top military honors, with burial in Arlington, attended by President Coolidge and most of the highest ranking dignitaries in Washington.

Hell, I thought, somebody must have written a book about this imposing character, even if we hadn't found one listed in the little Westminster library. Think of all those hundreds of Civil War books. I didn't suppose there was a single general, let alone major general, who hadn't been immortalized at least once by some college history prof or other. Even if only an old Ph.D. thesis, rehashed under a grant from Ford or Guggenheim, published by the University of North Branch, Nebraska.

I was even more confident there must be such a book, somewhere, after it dawned on me what it must have meant to be

11

called "general of the Army" from 1895 until 1903. Miles must have occupied the same position, all during the Spanish-American War, as that of Grant in the Civil War, Pershing in World War I, Marshall in World War II. "Commander-in-chief of all U.S. Armies" is one of several terms which have at various times been applied to the general officers in this capacity.

But it was to be some time after the Westminster history piece was written that, here and there, I would run across evidence of some of the real reasons why Miles had managed to get himself so thoroughly buried even long before he died. And how he could have held the top military post during a major war, without that fact's ever becoming generally known to the public, history teachers included.

After the library closed and I was headed homeward, back up into the New Hampshire hills—we live about fifty miles north of Westminster—I stopped off in Peterborough for a visit with Bill and Liz Bauhan. Bill has a small publishing business, and he had contracted to put out the history. This always made a good excuse to drop in for a conference and a spot of bourbon. Bill understands the great strain serious writers often feel by late afternoon, and he keeps a stock of proper remedies at hand.

I told Bill about my discovery of General Nelson A. Miles, amid the moldering trophies of ancient wars, in the well-concealed old museum room above the library. "Great!" he said, refilling my glass. "Maybe we ought to have a whole chapter about him, aside from the genealogy, I mean—the town hero, and all that—God knows we need *something* to liven it up." He grinned. "No reflection on your writing, of course."

"I'm with you," I agreed. "Special chapter, say, six to eight pages. But all they know down there about their most illustrious native son, and what I've found out so far, I could write in one paragraph. Mostly just the various ranks he held. Whether he was actually one of the greatest generals in American history, as his record seems to show on the face of it, or pretty much of a figurehead—maybe even just some old poop who didn't amount to a hill of beans—I still have no idea."

"Well, it doesn't matter." He poured another round. "Just go ahead and *imply* this chap was greater than Grant, Pershing, and MacArthur rolled into one. They'll love it."

"You insult my integrity," I said. "My devotion to hard, cold fact is well known to readers throughout the country— anyway, the country between here and the Massachusetts line. And by the way, Bill, you ought to remember something about Miles. Weren't you the whiz kid of American history in your Princeton days?"

But Bill could think of nothing more than that Miles had some connection with Puerto Rico during the Spanish-American War. He was quite incredulous when I told him our man had also been a major general in the Civil War and was still living by 1925. (I hadn't yet read about Miles' twenty-two years of service in the Indian campaigns.)

"Well, if this is all true," Bill said, "then it's ten to one there's some biographical stuff about him, if you can find it. Better try the Library of Congress."

And eventually I did. Or rather got my good friend Kay Fox, who presides down at the excellent library in Keene, our county seat, to do it for me. But the results were largely negative. For some reason, nobody had ever wanted to write much at all about the Nestor of American Army leaders, premier Indian fighter, diplomat, author, etc.

A couple of our more scholarly friends kindly explained how I could obtain all the information I wanted. Just run down to Washington and spend a few weeks going through the War Department archives, newspaper files, and so on. Accustomed as such people have now become to ample salaries, paid leaves, and grants and endowments, they didn't quite understand my position. The fact was, the history was just a part-time job, and the material was all supposed to be supplied; the budget didn't allow for any trips to Washington or anywhere else.

13

Then I learned that Nelson Miles' only son, Maj. Gen. Sherman Miles, though nearing eighty was still very much alive and living near Boston. A West Pointer and career Army man, he had been retired since sometime after World War II.

So I wrote Sherman Miles to see what information about his father he might contribute for the benefit of the Westminster history. His answer was impersonally polite and almost totally noncommittal. The implication was that I should be able to make out with whatever could be found in public records. It was about the most extreme example of military reserve—or something—I had ever run into.

It began to look more and more as though there must be a skeleton in the closet, or perhaps a whole stack of them. How else could you account for any man, who could reach the highest military post in the land, dropping so suddenly out of sight? And though he was still hale and hearty for more than twenty years after he retired?

At the time, my main thought about all this was that it was a petty annoyance. We were trying to meet the deadline set for getting the history to the printers. I just wanted enough facts for a well-rounded sketch of the old general; stating, with some accuracy, about where he should be placed as to his importance in military history. But everywhere I turned, I ran into crazy contradictions, wildly improbable theories, and a tangled web of political shenanigans. In short, a succession of mysteries.

It was the General himself who got me out of this hole. At least to the extent that I was able, in good conscience, to write a veritable paean of praise and flattery in six pages. And the Historical Society members were startled to find their forgotten general suddenly elevated to an eminence, in several respects, quite without parallel.

All the data we needed had been right there, all along, in the Westminster library. Remembering the reference to Miles as an "author," the next time I went down, I asked if they had any of his writings on hand. After some searching among the oldest shelves, the librarian came up with two large volumes of reminiscences. The first was published in 1896; the second, after the Spanish-American War. And between their long-unopened covers I found the elements of a story I hoped there would some day be time to tell in my own words—without the footnotes, index, bibliography, and all the other trappings of the devout, scholarly researcher.

Miles' role in American history, it seemed to me, fairly demanded that the story be brought up to date. For whatever he was, or was not, Miles *is* history. For my part, however, and I'm no historian, I happen to be most interested in him for his own sake—trying to find out just what kind of man he really was.

2

MOST of what is known about Miles' background, boyhood, and early manhood can be found in his first book. It was published by the Werner Company, Chicago and New York, in 1896, when the then just-appointed general of the Army was fifty-eight. This large, 590-page volume deserved at least honorable mention for its length of title, even in those days of florid, pompous mannerism.

PERSONAL RECOLLECTIONS
And Observations Of
GENERAL NELSON A. MILES
Embracing A Brief View Of The Civil War
OR
FROM NEW ENGLAND TO THE GOLDEN GATE
And The Story Of His Indian Campaigns
WITH COMMENTS ON THE
EXPLORATION, DEVELOPMENT AND PROGRESS
Of
OUR GREAT WESTERN EMPIRE

Copiously Illustrated With Graphic Pictures By
FREDERIC REMINGTON
And Other Eminent Artists

The farm where Nelson Appleton Miles was born in 1839 was even at that time an establishment that had seen its best days. Ambitious farmers had begun to move westward to more fertile lands. Townships like Westminster had already become largely industrialized. Most of the inhabitants still *lived* on farms, but only the poorest or the richest still managed without some other form of income. The poor made a subsistence living at best; the wealthy had inherited both money and those farms which were big enough, and good enough, to be able to survive profitably.

Daniel Miles' homestead was a modest frame house, with the usual outbuildings and perhaps a hundred acres of land, enough of it in tillage to support a few cows, horses, and assorted livestock. The place made a comfortable home and provided most of the provender needed for the family, but no real profit in terms of cash. Such money as there was came from Miles' small lumberyard in the village, where he spent most of his days.

Much of the farm work had to be done by the four children. So Nelson, the youngest, a remarkably rugged specimen from birth, could doubtless hardly remember when he first learned to handle an ax, milk cows, ride horses to work, help with the butchering, or set a box trap in the woods to catch hares.

Daniel Miles seems to have been a fairly typical Yankee countryman of his time, hardworking, pious, and well read for a self-educated farm boy, but with nothing about him of special interest which has survived. His wife, however, must have been unusually attractive and engaging, and in spite of leading a rather hard life, she was long remembered for the sort of charm one associates with true gentility, for lack of a better term. In any case, it would seem that from her Nelson inherited his dynamic good looks and personal magnetism.

The family funds were far from adequate for any form of higher education, and Nelson Miles left the farm at sixteen to try his hand at a business career in Boston. He never returned to farm life. But his farm background often reoccurs to me when I read of how a few years later he became perhaps the most skilled of all military frontiersmen—showing the troopers, nearly starved, how to butcher the frozen carcass of a buffalo or deer and make use of the hides for additional clothing; when big game was not to be found, how to snare birds and hares; how to repair a broken-down army wagon with ax-hewn timber; how to fashion a new harness from rawhide. Officers from town or city backgrounds didn't succeed very well in the Montana country, two or three hundred miles from the nearest stage road or trading post.

In Boston, Miles found a job in a hardware store. He had some notion of learning what was then called the mercantile trade and had visions of soon making a fortune. For two or three years he worked hard toward this end, taking business courses at night school and saving as much as he could from a meager salary.

But more and more the agitation of the times began to absorb his interest. And as war became an imminent possibility, he decided to turn all his energies in that direction. By this time, Miles believed in the cause of abolition with all the fanaticism of youth. Another inducement came from an ardent hobby he had indulged since earliest school days—the reading of military histories and anything pertaining to military science. He had wanted to go to West Point, but it became obvious to him that he could never afford it.

In order to understand the very extraordinary circumstances that enabled Nelson Miles, at barely twenty-one, to be accepted by the Army as a first lieutenant, some conjectures must be made. There are few recorded facts about the personal life of the farm boy from Westminster during those five years, from age sixteen to twenty-one, he spent in Boston.

In the first place, the term "farm boy," as used in the General's brief and impersonal account of his youth, is somewhat misleading. This was no shy, uneducated rustic, come to the big city to make his way without contacts. The Miles family was cultured and well read, and Nelson had acquired at the Westminster Academy what for those days was a very good basic education. He had relatives in Boston, and in his business career and further studies he was helped by an uncle, his mother's brother. He could also maintain fairly close relations with family and friends at home. Westminster was only an hour or so from Boston by train. It was even easier, then, to travel from downtown Boston to Westminster than it is in today's heavy traffic.

Miles may well have been an unusually reserved and quiet lad when it came to the purely social side of life. But he was certainly not shy or slow to express himself, in any company, on subjects that interested him. It was a man's world, as he saw it then. He was fascinated with national politics and all the implications of a rapidly approaching war between the states. His most passionate interest was military science, and his idea of sport was almost anything that involved violent outdoor activity. He thought nothing of hiking the 45 miles between Boston and home, on occasion, to save carfare; a walk that, in fact, was hardly more than a mild exercise for his powerful six-foot-two frame.

By the summer of 1860 the feeling was becoming quite general in New England, and especially in the abolitionist intellectual community of Boston, that war was inevitable. Nelson Miles, the student of military tactics, was of no mind to find himself caught in the role of a mere private soldier. What he did about it is outlined in a paragraph from the *Recollections*:

Together with a few young men in Boston I placed myself under the tutelage of an old French colonel named Salignac, and all the time I could find available was devoted to the study and practice of military drills, the duties of officers, discipline, and the methods of command and administration. This French officer was most thorough in all his methods and action, and the corps of young men under his instruction finally grew from a

19

single small company until it numbered first and last, over three thousand men. By him were schooled a very large number of the men who afterwards became officers of Massachusetts regiments.

After war was declared in April, 1861, Miles quit his job and gave full time to his military studies. The following summer, when Congress asked for 500,000 volunteers to support the hard-pressed regular Army, he decided to recruit a hand-picked company in hopes of being elected its captain.

He had no trouble finding enough men, for the enthusiasm to "defend the Union" amounted to hysteria at the time, and recruiting centers were being jammed. It was common practice to organize volunteer companies privately in this manner. But it might be guessed that rarely, if ever, was such a group led by one so young. (One is here reminded that when Theodore Roosevelt recruited his Rough Riders in 1898, though he was youthfully depicted by the popular magazines of the day, he was forty-one.)

We can only imagine the self-confidence, the personality traits, the magnetic attraction, that would inspire such faith in Miles when he was barely of voting age. But the matter of money was not so easy for him. Volunteer outfits had to pay their own way until such time as they might be accepted into the Union command. (The practice continued until after the Spanish-American War, when the National Guard system became less independent.) To equip and pay his men during the initial period of organizing and training cost Miles $3,500. He put up his own total savings of $1,000 and borrowed $2,500. It was expected that such expenses would eventually be made good by the government, but Miles was never to be reimbursed.

By September, Miles had been formally chosen captain by his well-drilled recruits, his popularity evidently unchallenged among the men. His rank was approved, and the company was inducted into the 22nd Massachusetts Regiment. Then the young officer, out of the blue, was handed his first real setback. He received a note from the governor of Massachusetts, who was required to sign all commissions of volunteers, saying a mistake had been made: the captain's commission was to be returned and a lieutenant's commission would be issued instead.

It seemed the governor had a friend who was looking for a captain's commission the easy way. Miles protested with rather more anger than diplomacy. The governor replied that he was forced to cancel the captain's commission when he discovered Miles was, in his judgment, too young to hold such a rank.

The night before the regiment was to leave for the South, the governor sent Miles his signed lieutenant's commission and required the return of the captain's certification. Miles had no further choice. As he wrote later, he preferred to go to the front as a demoted captain rather than stay home and fight the governor. So it seems the present well-known Massachusetts brand of politics was operating more than a century ago.

I have no intention of setting down here anything like a week-by-week account of Miles' next three years, to the end of the Civil War in 1865. For one thing, that would take another 500 pages; for another, numerous Civil War histories have traced Miles' battle exploits in detail from Seven Pines to Appomattox. So, with this apology to all Civil War buffs, we will proceed with this phase of the Miles story boiled down to a factual outline, without benefit of Rebel yells, singing "Dixie" round the campfire, and Robert E. Lee sitting astride Traveler in the fading sunset.

Miles himself, when later writing his *Recollections*, seems to have felt that even then the history books had adequately covered his Civil War career. He compressed his account of the war into a dozen pages, only in part dealing with his own adventures. Then he went on to devote 400 pages to his twenty-two years of Indian fighting in the West.

Miles admitted frankly that in the impending war he saw a chance to realize his great dream of an Army officer's career, something he had long thought impossible because he couldn't afford West Point. It was to this end he studied so hard with Salignac for several months instead of enlisting at the start of the war.

But it would be unfair to accuse him of opportunism, in the light of his later well-known habit of publicly and loudly damning any war that he thought unjustified or avoidable. Furthermore, in the Civil War, the decision to try to win promotion by getting into the front ranks was much more apt to lead to getting killed than ever reaching a general's rank.

Miles' first concern was to get transferred from his Massachusetts regiment. He had no desire to serve under the man who had usurped his captaincy, nor was the governor likely to allow him to be promoted. During the fall he was detailed for a few weeks to serve as aide-de-camp, then moved to assistant adjutant general of a brigade. And beginning with the battle of Seven Pines, he was in the thick of the fighting in several engagements.

Miles was soon recommended for promotion, but as he was still with the Massachusetts Volunteers, and the same governor was still in office, nothing came of it. Then, at the end of May, 1862, he was appointed lieutenant colonel of the 61st New York Volunteers. The colonel, Francis Barlow, had seen Miles assume command and rally some badly disorganized units in a critical situation at the Battle of Malvern Hill. Barlow persuaded New York's governor Edwin D. Morgan to endorse a commission for Miles as second in command in his regiment from that state. Both Barlow and the commanding general, Edwin Sumner, were much impressed with Miles' talent for tactics and his courage in several subsequent battles. In September, when Barlow was promoted to brigadier general, Miles succeeded him as colonel.

During the next two years Miles was wounded twice. The first time, at Marye's Heights, a "Minnie" ball tore into his neck and just missed his jugular vein. He stayed in the field for a time, holding his wounded neck, but was finally carried to the rear and hospitalized. In a few weeks he recovered and was back in action. The second wound, at Chancellorsville, was so severe he was not expected to live—a punctured abdomen and fractured hipbone. Abdominal wounds were almost always fatal in those days.

But Miles was apparently indestructible and impervious to infection. He was shipped back to Massachusetts, but after several weeks of recuperating he was able to get out on crutches, and he headed back toward the front. He was not allowed to resume his command for two or three months, but spent the rest of his convalescing period in a program of training for local Pennsylvania volunteers. This was before Gettysburg; it was feared Lee's army would advance all the way through Pennsylvania, and home defense militia units were hurriedly being organized.

Late in 1863 Miles was able to resume his command of the 61st New York Volunteers. And in May, 1864, he was promoted to brigadier general. In August he was made brevet major general, i.e., acting in this capacity as a field commander. And finally, early in 1865, the rank of major general was confirmed; Miles was in command of the 1st Division, 2nd Army Corps. (Previously commanded in turn by Couch, Hancock, Sedgwick, French, Hayes, Mott, Barlow, Caldwell, and Humphries.) Just before the close of the war, he was for a short time commander of the whole 2nd Army Corps, by far the youngest corps commander in the Civil War or any war since.

I have run across many references to Nelson A. Miles as "the youngest major general in the Civil War," and about as many naming George A. Custer for the same honor. The duality seems to stem from several rather ambiguous factors. Miles was almost four months the older man, Custer having been born December 5, 1839.

Should we use the dates of when the commissions were issued, or when they were received? Perhaps we should decide the question on the basis of which man was first brevetted, prior to receiving official notification of rank. On these points there is some difference of opinion, and some doubts about fixing exact dates. In the Civil War officers were often advanced verbally by their superiors on the battlefields; even high-ranking general officers, incapacitated or killed in action, would be replaced on the field with the most likely candidates at hand. If they were retained, the papers confirming their advanced rank might take days or weeks to be delivered to them.

Still further confusion may have resulted from the fact that Custer was a West Point graduate and a regular Army officer, while Miles was a member of the volunteers. The two types of service did not employ the same methods of promotion and were often at odds about what should be considered official and proper. For my part, I don't really care which was the younger major general, Miles or Custer. Let the history buffs fight it out. But I will stress the point that Miles was beyond doubt the youngest major general ever to be entrusted with command of a whole army corps.

3

MORE than thirty years later, when Miles became a victim of jingoist politicians and certain chain newspapers that set an all-time record for yellow journalism, he was insulted and generally kicked around by some powerful enemies, including Presidents McKinley and Roosevelt. Much of the vilification has been repeated, in "historical" books of one sort or another, even up to the past ten years, as we will show in subsequent pages. But though Miles' jealous opponents at times seemed capable of stopping at nothing, however unwarranted, to belittle his military accomplishments, none ever dared to attack his Civil War record. None, at least, that I've been able to find.

The farm boy lieutenant from Massachusetts had entered the war without influence or resources or much in the way of formal education. He emerged at the end with a reputation for leadership that had come to the attention of the Secretary of War and such military elite as Grant, Sherman, Sheridan, and Hancock. He had received the Medal of Honor, and his major general's rank had been won solely through such exploits as holding his regiment's position at Reams Station while the rest of the Union forces fell back in confusion. His record of promotions had been equaled only by the West Point-trained Custer.

With characteristic ambition and self-confidence, Miles

didn't wait for his reputation to cool off at the end of the war before applying for a regular Army commission. And as usual he aimed high. Collecting personal recommendations from Grant, Sherman, and others, he put in for the rank of brigadier general.

For this, certain less successful West Pointers, who had a poor opinion of volunteers generally, accused him later of egotism and undue self-interest. But it must be considered that at the time, the Union Armies numbered about a million and a half men. Nobody, let alone Miles, could foresee how much, or how soon, that force would be reduced after the war. His request for a brigadier general's post would look presumptuous only after it became known the Army was being suddenly cut down to only 50,000 men, and soon after to 30,000, thus leaving room for only 17 general officers in all (the commanding general of the Army, a lieutenant general, 10 brigadiers, and 5 major generals).

Miles was, however, granted a regular Army commission as a full colonel, which was remarkable enough. Many older general officers had to settle for major's rank. Custer was reduced to lieutenant colonel. In the months following the surrender, while many of the volunteer forces were not yet disbanded, Miles was sent to command the post of Fort Monroe.

There had recently been a great hue and cry raised for the "punishment" of former Confederate President Jefferson Davis. Spurred on by scurrilous newspapers, rabble-rousing politicians, and some Northern fanatics, the government decided to set the military on the trail of the fugitive. They caught up with poor Davis as he was trying to make his way, incognito, by horse and buggy, to some Southern port where he might escape to foreign parts.

Davis was brought up to Fort Monroe and there placed in the custody of Miles, who was ordered to keep him under maximum security. Hardly had this been done when Southern sympathizers in Washington went into action, and the same

26

newspapers which had shouted for Davis' arrest now claimed he was being tortured. He was said to be confined in a dark dungeon, "in irons," ill and half-starved.

Nothing could have been further from the truth. Miles, always the stickler for military protocol and anxious to make a good impression for his men as well as for himself, was treating Davis with every comfort and courtesy the fort could afford, and Davis was in good health. As for the irons, some reporter had seen a chance to make a good story from hearsay that Miles had been ordered to handcuff the prisoner for a short time, while his quarters were being fitted with proper locks and bars.

Miles sent emphatic reports to the War Department denying the tales about mistreating Davis and offering unimpeachable proofs and witnesses to bear him out. But the reports were ignored. President Johnson's weak and intimidated cabinet advisers decided they needed a scapegoat to quiet the Davis affair. Miles was removed from command of Monroe, ostensibly because of his "mistreatment" of Davis.

Coming so soon after all the glory and acclaim as a Union war hero, the young officer was probably nearer to being discouraged than at any time in his life. But there was nothing he could do except to fall back on his status as a regular Army colonel (previously approved, fortunately) and await further orders.

All the evidence we have suggests that Nelson Miles, at twenty-six, impressed everybody who knew him with one basic trait of his character above all else in his reserved personality and handsomely striking appearance—self-assurance. Self-assurance so complete, so natural and unassumed, it needed no expression through the histrionics affected by such contemporaries as Gen. George Crook, Indian scout Bill Cody, or the dashing Custer.

The trait seems inherent in the Miles family, but in Nelson's case the tremendously intense experiences of the Civil

War crystallized it into an almost mystical faith in his own destiny. In rapid succession he had seen many all-powerful commanders, like McClellan, lose their authority and their reputations overnight due to moments of self-doubt or indecision in some single important battle.

Miles' basic military philosophy was simple. Never overlook anything, from a field gun to a shoelace, in training and outfitting for even the most minor skirmish. Never relax because of having an apparently overwhelming advantage. Never leave an important decision to a subordinate if it can be avoided. Always study everything that can be learned in advance about the enemy's psychology and tactics.

The philosophy may not have been unique, but the length to which Miles would go to carry it out was, to say the least, unusual. Especially for a young junior officer. If he thought an order received from a superior was unsound or unwise, or merely unfair according to his rigid tenets of behavior, he would try to get around it by some means or other, even though the order might have come from the President himself. It was a habit that led, quite naturally, to a rather widespread impression that he was utterly unimpressed by any title except his own.

In a later time, we have seen public opinion sharply divided with respect to a similarly famous and colorful military figure, Gen. Douglas MacArthur. There are the endless anecdotes, both true and invented, repeated by those convinced that he was arrogant and vain; and there are those who are equally sure he was never motivated by the slightest self-interest. But there has been little room for argument regarding MacArthur's outstanding military ability, and his success and popularity in carrying out the Army occupation of Japan.

In the case of the youthful Miles, he was of course bound to be judged in the light of the social mores of that late Victorian period. It was not a time when frankness of the Miles brand, or of any brand for that matter, was generally popular. Protocol was more important than performance in the U.S. military hierarchy, except when the very survival of the country was at stake.

I have gone into this aspect of the Miles character—self-assurance versus arrogance—when we are thinking of him at age twenty-six, not only because it explains the course and shape of his later career. It also has a great deal of bearing on the strange way he has been treated by historians, even to the present day. Miles' direct way of expressing himself and his method of dealing head-on with any situation in which his considered opinion was opposed showed no sign of change throughout his long life. Miles never "mellowed with age." His interests broadened into many fields, but his new-Federalist approach to thought and action remained as constant as his daily outdoor exercise.

In the Miles view of life's whole spectrum, wrong was black and right was white—no shading, no neutral ground. Even in private, intimate letters to his family, he was fond of sentences such as: "There has been no branch of our government so corrupt and disgraceful to the Republic as that which has had the management of our Indian affairs."

Following the unfortunate business at Fort Monroe, Miles was ordered to North Carolina where Gen. Oliver O. Howard was commissioner of the Freedmen's Bureau, a sort of army of occupation set up to aid Southern states in reconstruction (ostensibly at least), oversee the adopting and enforcing of new constitutions, etc. Miles was enthusiastic about the work and had no use for the high-handed methods of certain officers engaged in reconstruction in other Southern states. Certainly a more effective job seems to have been done in North Carolina, but how much of this was due to Miles himself can only be conjectured.

Miles was lucky to be an aide of Howard, under whom he had served in the war until after the Seven Pines battle. It was in that fight that Miles had continued to rally his regi-

29

ment after he was wounded in the neck, and Howard had been so impressed he might have managed to get the young lieutenant promoted. But the next day Howard had lost an arm and was out of action, and Miles soon after had been transferred to the New York Volunteers.

On furlough to the North in 1867, Miles was invited to visit friends in Cleveland. There he met the extremely attractive and popular daughter of Judge Charles Sherman. The Sherman family was about as prominent in Ohio, at that time, as the Tafts were to become a couple of generations later. Judge Sherman was a commissioner of the Union Pacific Railroad, among other things; his brother John was a well-known U.S. Senator; another brother was William Tecumseh, of Civil War fame, commander-in-chief of the Army after Grant became President.

Nelson Miles had become something of a ladies' man, in his own rather reserved and formal way. On leaves in Washington and Boston he had been surprised to find himself in great demand among the leading hostesses of the social register set. As a returning war hero, his almost unbelievable good looks and his naturally courtly manner attracted quite a following among the current debutantes.

But Mary Sherman was the first girl Miles really fell in love with. As for the details of the romance, we can only guess. Miles' Yankee reticence about such personal matters was so great that in his *Recollections* we only learn of his marriage when he comes to describe frontier life and mentions a visit from his wife. (All his voluminous letters to her were kept by his son, Gen. Sherman Miles, and none were released until 1960.)

In any case, events soon after they met make it quite plain that for this couple it was love at first sight. Mary told her parents, after he had returned to North Carolina, that she was corresponding with Nelson daily and she was entirely sure of her feelings for him.

Judge Sherman did some investigating through such channels as his friend Senator Charles Sumner of Massachusetts. All reports were satisfactory to the judge and his wife. Within a few months Miles wrote a formal letter to Mary's father, requesting permission for her hand in marriage. And if it was possible for Nelson Miles to feel fear (an admittedly debatable question) he must have felt it then; for it was probably the only formal communication he ever wrote in his life, after entering the Army, without adding his rank to his signature. This time he just ended with "Your obt. Svt, Nelson A. Miles, U.S.A."

They were married June 30, 1868. The Cleveland social scene was dominated by an array of full-dress uniforms never equaled there before or since. As General Sherman was the uncle of the bride, most of the top army brass had been invited, including Grant.

Less than a year later, Miles was ordered West to serve in the Indian campaigns. The entire system of Indian reservations and the administration of Indian affairs had broken down, and the Army was being sent out to round up the marauding tribes. It was thought that the primitive Indians, with their bows and arrows, would be no match for the concentrated forces of the U.S. cavalry and infantry. Nobody could imagine it was the start of a savage war, in many ways unparalleled in military history, which would take more than twenty years to finish.

FOR a period of about twenty-five years, roughly from 1850 to 1875, the boundary between the civilized and settled East and the still undeveloped West remained quite static. Commonly called "the frontier," it ran northward along the Mississippi to St. Louis, then branched slightly farther west along the Missouri. Above the eastern end of Nebraska, as the Missouri turns more to the west through the Dakotas, the frontier continued on northward more or less along the western border of Minnesota.

This meant that nearly two thirds of the total area of the United States was still very largely undeveloped wilderness. Travel and commerce between the thin line of the settled area along the West coast and the Eastern states depended on shipping which had to go around South America via Cape Horn. Work on transcontinental rail lines was begun west of the frontier after the Civil War. All railroads built earlier had ended at either the Mississippi or the Missouri.

So, at the start of the Indian campaigns, the rebellious tribes could wander at will over the whole vast territory comprising Texas, Oklahoma, Kansas, Nebraska, the Dakotas, New Mexico, Colorado, Wyoming, Montana, Arizona, Utah, Idaho, Washington, Nevada, Oregon, and parts of California.

There was, of course, a great deal of more or less isolated development going on in all these states and future states.

The advent of large numbers of white settlers, after the Civil War, had in fact precipitated the Indian rebellions, for the whites staked out their villages and homesteads without regard to the boundaries of Indian reservations and hunting grounds. But all travel was by wagon train, horseback, or foot. In mobility, the Indians had a great advantage over the white man. Those tribes not inherently nomadic had become so as they were driven ever farther westward.

Civilians in the government who controlled the War Department in Washington were blissfully ignorant of the character and vastness of the regions involved and hadn't the slightest idea of the Indians' capacity for waging war. The generals sent West to command the Army forces were veterans of the Civil War, but that experience did them little good when they found themselves several hundred miles from any source of supplies, doing battle with an enemy using tactics that were never taught at West Point. It would take several years for the high command to learn even the simple and obvious ground rule that infantry forces, in a country without roads or supply lines, were practically useless against mounted Indians who were among the world's greatest horsemen.

Such was the general state of affairs when Miles, in the spring of 1869, arrived at Fort Hays, Kansas, headquarters of the 5th U.S. Infantry. Hays was quite far out on the wild, windswept Kansas plains, in the heart of the buffalo country. Even the officers' quarters were crude shacks, with outdoor toilets, stoves that hardly kept the rooms above freezing in severe winter weather, and no running water. There was, however, a rather jerry-built rail line running out from Leavenworth, the main Western Army headquarters at the eastern edge of Kansas.

A few hardy wives of officers managed to keep house at Hays, and Mary Miles insisted on going out with her husband to his new command. Fortunately it was nearly April when they arrived. Miles, with his farm background, was no stranger to the intricacies of heating and cooking with woodburning stoves and fireplaces. From all accounts, he kept his young bride reasonably comfortable as well as inspiring her to share his excited enthusiasm for frontier life—riding, hunting, fishing, and exploring.

In addition to the rigors of housekeeping at Fort Hays, there was some feeling of tension—especially on the part of the wives—because of the ever present chance of "hostiles" being nearby. Most of the Indians they saw were friendly. But from time to time, warriors who had been captured in skirmishes with marauding tribes were brought in and imprisoned in a sort of compound. There were some attempted outbreaks, rioting, and several killings; and it was sometimes impossible to be sure which Indians were friendly and which were not.

Besides the 5th Infantry post, there was also, a little way outside the cluster of saloons and other frame buildings then known as Hays City, the encampment of the 7th Cavalry. This unit was commanded by Col. George Armstrong Custer (brevet major general). Custer had been campaigning out of Fort Hays for the past year or so and already had made quite a name for himself as an Indian fighter. Inevitably, after the massacre of 1876, he was to become forever a subject for debate in military history. But in the preceding years he was rated very highly by his superiors. And from Texas to the Canadian border, wherever there was bad Indian trouble in some remote area, Custer's outfit was a favored choice to go out and pursue the hostiles.

George Custer was a reporter's dream come true, and most journalists covering frontier life made the most of it. Artists and photographers found him the archetype of the dashing Western-style cavalryman—he had long, blond, wavy hair, sweeping moustache, and handsome features, and when off duty, he wore the picturesque buckskins of the plainsman. He was a spectacular horseman and a crack shot, and was fond of

34

big-game hunting, especially the dangerous sport of shooting buffalo from horseback.

Whenever possible, Custer was accompanied by his young wife, Elizabeth. In later years she wrote extensively and also lectured about her Western adventures. Elizabeth Custer and Mary Miles had much in common and became good friends. Elizabeth was already a veteran of frontier living when the Mileses arrived at Hays, and she did a great deal to make Mary's first months there a happy experience. Both girls were good riders, and they often went along with their husbands on hunting and exploring expeditions.

Miles liked Custer personally and soon came to have a high regard for his knowledge of Western geography and his ability as an officer in maintaining a high standard of discipline and efficiency. He was frankly envious of Custer's accomplishments and reputation, and learned as much as he could from firsthand accounts of the cavalryman's several battles with the Indians. He was impatient for a chance to get into action with his own command.

But the summer went by with no such chance, and then Miles was shifted to Leavenworth. For the next three years the ambitious young colonel was totally frustrated in all efforts to be sent out to any area where he might see some fighting.

To offset the discouragement Miles felt at what seemed a hopeless bogging down of his military career, there was his enormous happiness with Mary. Their first child, Cecelia, had been born in 1869, and at Leavenworth the officers' quarters were comfortable and well-equipped modern houses. Mary was happy and contented there. She was proving to be the ideal army wife, a distinction she was to carry for the rest of her life. From the first, she never had the slightest doubt that General, as she was fond of calling her husband, was the ablest commander in the whole U.S. Army.

But whenever Mary tried to impress this opinion on her

Uncle Cump—General of the Army William T. Sherman—she ran into a stone wall. Sherman was fond of his relatives, but even fonder of Army regulations and custom. He was a fanatical believer in the seniority system and actually felt that any deviation from it would lead to undermining the whole integrity of the Army.

Miles saw himself as a victim of nepotism in reverse. Sherman would never promote him, it seemed, on the basis of ability, knowledge, and hard work; and as a nephew-in-law, he wasn't going to be shown any special favor by the crusty old general. Whenever a promotion did occur, it went to some older West Pointer, and Miles thought some who had been made division commanders had little but age to recommend them for service in the Western wilderness. About the only consolation he had was that the highly publicized and popular Custer, his chief rival, also continued to be held down to the rank of colonel.

As later events turned out, it may have been the best thing that could have happened to Miles that he was kept on duty at Leavenworth those three years. He was able to learn a great deal there about the background of the Indian situation, the Indians themselves, and the scouts and guides and other Western characters who knew them best.

Leavenworth was the principal jumping-off place not only for Army units going West, but for emigrant wagon trains and all sorts of travelers and adventurers. There were many prospectors and a good share of desperadoes and prostitutes. Except for the occasional danger of Indian trouble, the great Western territories were wide open, and the vast migration was reaching a peak. It was rather like a continuous race to "get out there"—wherever "there" might be—ahead of the railroads and the developers.

It was also the peak period for buffalo hunting. The next twenty years would see the greatest slaughter of big game in history, with millions of animals killed, ending in almost

36

total extinction of the bison species. The situation at Leavenworth was similar to what happened at Nairobi in the 1930's, when East Africa, then still colonial, became a dream of every big-game hunter, with a dead elephant the supreme reward.

There was nothing quite like the American bison. Collectively the animals behaved like vast herds of wild cattle, roaming and grazing over the Great Plains. But when one of the beasts was overtaken or cornered, it would turn on the hunter with about as much ferocity as a charging rhino. There was also always the danger that a densely packed herd of many thousands would suddenly stampede, trampling down anything in its path, even to a whole encampment of emigrating settlers.

During untold ages, before the Spanish explorers left the Plains Indians the accidental legacy of horses, very few buffalo could be killed by hunters. The only checks on the population of the herds were natural predators and the extent of grazing lands, chiefly the latter. As the Indians began using horses (the only benefit the Indian ever derived from the white man, it appears, in some four centuries) they developed a highly skilled and effective means of hunting. Horses were faster than buffalo for short distances. Individuals could be cut out from the herds and killed with spears, and in later years, with guns.

But the Indians still did not kill nearly enough buffalo to deplete the herds. They killed mainly for meat and such hides as they needed for robes and tepees. It remained for the whites to slaughter great numbers for sport alone, leaving the carcasses to rot where they fell. As soon as the railroads reached as far out as the edge of the Kansas plains, two new types of hunters began to arrive. The first were the dudes, the second the market hunters.

A dude was anybody from the East or abroad who came West not as a settler, and usually not to prospect or gamble or rob stagecoaches, but usually as a sportsman, artist, writer, naturalist, or just sightseer. There were even a few female dudes. The exploits of Isabella Bird, an aristocratic English lady who wore a bloomer suit and rode man-style, packing a six-gun, inspired all sorts of gossip and tall tales the length of the frontier. One of the more fascinating was quite true— her romance with one-eyed Mountain Jim Nugent, a celebrated guide and woodsman.

In the East, there was a great promotion of books and articles about buffalo hunting, some authentic and many spurious, usually illustrated with paintings or photographs. Many wealthy European sportsmen were attracted by the tales of Western hunting and came over to have a try at collecting a few trophies. Most impressive dude of all was the Russian Grand Duke Alexis Aleksandrovich. He took the field with an entourage of a hundred or so—servants, friends, and an Army escort—and his safari was conducted by General Sheridan. Custer was detailed to show him how to shoot buffalo.

Hunting was a favorite sport of both Custer and Miles. Miles was at least Custer's equal as a horseman and a rifle shot, but he was much too conscientious to take as much time off for hunting as was the habit of his carefree cavalry friend.

Knowing how to find and kill a buffalo could mean the difference between survival and starvation for an army unit stranded hundreds of miles from a supply base. But Miles was appalled at the extent market-hunting was being carried on all over the plains country. He estimated more than a million buffalo were killed in one year. Contractors supplying the rail crews with meat wasted hides and removed only the choice steaks, and gangs of hide hunters left all the meat. Calves from stampeded herds were butchered wholesale for the tenderer veal, leaving no stock for reproduction. Years later, a bone-meal concern would find it profitable to harvest hundreds of tons of whitened skeletons littering the ground in some areas.

A story was told about Buffalo Bill (William F. Cody), most

famous of all frontiersmen, and one of his rivals then engaged in market-hunting for the railroads. The competitor claimed the reports of Cody's marksmanship had been stretched considerably. Buffalo Bill challenged the man to a duel in the form of a day's shoot, to see who could kill the most buffalo. The count at sundown credited Buffalo Bill with a score of 67, the other hunter with 43.

At Leavenworth, Miles became well acquainted with Buffalo Bill, who was then in his late twenties and well known throughout the West, aside from his buffalo hunting exploits, as a guide and an expert on Indian life and behavior. He had actually lived with the Indians for much of his boyhood. A natural showman and spinner of tall yarns, there were many who doubted his authenticity. But Miles was convinced Cody knew a great deal about the finer distinctions between the various tribes: which ones were friendly and which could not be trusted; and how to communicate and deal with Indians generally. Later Miles was to hire him as an Army scout, a decision greatly affecting the careers of both men.

Miles was a student of human nature, in his own self-taught and highly individual way, and he had a strong philosophical bent. His view of the whole Indian situation, even before he became actively engaged in it, was almost unique for a military man of his time. It was one of his cardinal tenets that to fight an enemy effectively, one should know all that could be learned about that enemy's character and psychology, and above all, the enemy's *reason* for fighting.

General Sherman regarded Indians only as an elusive nuisance that constantly plagued his official position. They were an inferior race of savages, and he would willingly have had them all exterminated. Sheridan, in charge of all Western operations and Sherman's eventual successor, held much the same view. But for practical purposes, he and his division commanders had learned there were two kinds of Indians—good ones and bad ones.

The good ones were the tribes and individuals willing to cooperate, in greater or lesser degree, with the Army—those who could be hired or coerced into making war against their own kind. The bad ones—notably the Sioux, Cheyennes, Nez Perces, and Apaches—were those who, when pushed far enough by the white man, had sufficient spirit and intelligence left to launch an all-out war of retaliation.

Miles' thinking was, in a sense, the reverse of that of his colleagues and his superiors, and for a long time it did not help his popularity or his chances for promotion. He admired and respected the tribes and their chiefs who, when their lands were stolen from them, their treaties with the government repeatedly broken, and their people reduced to starvation by corrupt reservation agents, decided to fight it out. Moreover, he regarded the "friendly Indians" who could be pushed around by the whites as useful to the Army at times but obviously inferior in character. Worst of all, he persisted in the unpopular notion that Indians were not a subhuman species but were entitled to equal rights with the whites as citizens; and that when defeated in battle, they should be treated honorably as prisoners of war and subsequently rehabilitated. The officially favored course of action was to shoot as many as possible on one pretext or another and jail the rest as common criminals.

Since Miles never hesitated to make his views loudly heard, he might never have been allowed to take a command into action, it is safe to say, if the failures of others had not aroused public opinion to the point that Sherman was getting desperate. The heat was being applied to Sherman directly from the White House. Congressmen from every Western state, and influential people from the territories, were demanding Army protection against the Indians. They were supported by the powerful railroad lobbies and the extensive mining and ranching interests.

Sherman would have liked an annual military appropriation at least three times greater than it was, and an increase in the size of the Army. But Congress was completely apathetic to any such plan. Sherman had to continue to rely on a total of only a dozen or so general officers, mostly brigadiers. Of these, only two, George Crook and Oliver Otis Howard, were at all effective at leading their troops in the wilderness. The rest were too old to stand the great physical hardships, or too inexperienced to be of any use in actual Indian-style fighting, or just not inclined to leave the security and comfort of their various headquarters posts.

So the forces that were sent out into the field, sometimes on extended campaigns of weeks or months, were commanded by colonels, majors, captains, and often even by lieutenants. The Army had to be distributed so widely that even the larger units usually mustered only a few hundred men.

Meanwhile the Indians were on the move and often joining together in increasing numbers. The situation was such that there was always a chance that any one of these Army expeditions, a hundred or more miles from its nearest support, might encounter a band of several thousand hostiles. This was foreseen by a few enlightened field officers such as Miles. But it would take a disaster of such magnitude as the Custer massacre, a couple of years later, to impress the facts of life on Washington and the War Department. And even that event produced wildly conflicting and unrealistic official reactions.

There was little about frontier life and frontier characters of all kinds that Miles hadn't learned after his two or three years at Leavenworth and other posts in the area. The wildest horse operas of the next century would hardly be able to outdo the reality of those times. Brawls, gunfights, and general lawlessness were the order of the day in what was perhaps the world's most hard-drinking society. Career Army officers were seldom immune to this environment. Miles had a good deal of trouble with the officers under his command, and at times with his superiors, in the matter of drunkenness and laxness of one sort or another.

For his own part, Miles was no puritan. Off the post, he would take a social drink or two with his harder-drinking friends often enough to avoid being called a prude. But his main interest was always in improving the training and efficiency of the 5th Infantry. He kept on hoping for a chance to go into action and demonstrate that his hard work and discipline would pay off, perhaps even more in Indian fighting than in conventional warfare. It seemed nothing else would ever induce Sherman to put his name up for promotion.

The chance finally came in 1874, with the start of what became known as the Kiowa-Comanche Campaign. Buffalo hunters and others had moved into the Indian territory, and the Kiowas and Comanches, joined by some Cheyennes, decided to go on the warpath and drive out the settlers.

Fighting began at Adobe Walls, in the desolate Staked Plains country of the Texas Panhandle, near the southeast and southwest corners of Colorado and Kansas, respectively. The Indians attacked a large camp of buffalo hide hunters. The plainsmen put up a good fight and finally the Indians withdrew, but it was thought that Adobe Walls could not hold out long without Army protection, and the place was evacuated for the time being.

As usual, the rights of the Indians to their own assigned lands were ignored when the news reached Washington. Settlers in Colorado, Kansas, Texas, and Indian territory had to be safeguarded against further raids. Sherman, at his St. Louis headquarters, was ordered to employ as many Army units as might be necessary to thoroughly whip the Indians.

5

RANKING second to General of the Army Sherman was Lt. Gen. Philip Sheridan, commanding the Division of the Missouri. Sheridan ordered four separate forces to converge in the general area where the hostiles were at large. From New Mexico, Major Price with four cavalry troops; from Texas, Colonel Mackenzie with another cavalry unit; from eastern Indian Territory, Colonel Davidson's command; and from Kansas, Colonel Miles with a battalion of the 5th and two cavalry battalions. Miles also took along a light artillery unit, some friendly Delaware Indians, and carefully chosen guides and scouts. As to the latter, Miles wrote his wife just before leaving Fort Dodge: "I find no trouble in getting all that class of men I want, and though they are a rough set of individuals they will be valuable for what I want them for."

It was this matter of selecting scouts and guides and knowing how to handle them which would, as much as anything else, set Miles in a class apart from all other field officers throughout the Indian campaigns. From the high command down to the ill-fated Custer, most of the West Point and Eastern-trained commanders never learned the full importance of this aspect of Indian warfare.

In preparing for his expedition against the Kiowas and Comanches, Miles also made use of a strategy that was to become his trademark—a careful assessment of the capabilities of the other forces in the campaign besides his own, and their commanding officers' past records. By this means he could predict with remarkable accuracy the movement and timing of another command and how it would react to whatever type of action might be encountered. The only possible communication among the various forces once they had gone into the field was by courier, uncertain at best. Therefore it was interesting to have such foreknowledge of a certain fellow officer as how well he trained and disciplined his men, how fast he could move in unknown country, and how prone he was to attack or retreat in the face of contact with a strong enemy force.

Of course this was only sound military thinking, of the sort which could have prevented several fatal ambushes that had occurred from time to time, as Miles had noted. But he had another reason for employing it. He was determined, in his first Indian campaign, that his own command would be ahead of the others in engaging the hostiles. Then he would be able to show that his men were the best-trained outfit in the whole Army of the West. Not that he intended to take any chance that could be avoided or fail to make use of whatever support was available. He just wanted to be first on the scene of action and to retain personal control of the campaign as a whole wherever possible. For this he was quite naturally labeled a glory hunter by many of his rivals for promotion.

So from the outset of the Kiowa-Comanche campaign, Miles was determined that forced marching, lack of proper supply trains, or other handicaps would not prevent his own command from playing the major part. He felt that Colonel Davidson's command would not arrive in time to accomplish much, and he knew Davidson had a rather poor record in his past dealings with the territory Indians he was supposed to control. Major Price he regarded, from what he had heard, as an ill-trained blunderer. Colonel Mackenzie's Texas command was another matter. Mackenzie was reputed to be a bold, aggressive Indian fighter of considerable experience, and he enjoyed the confidence of the division commander. But Miles knew him to be erratic and lacking in judgment. (He later became insane.) Miles figured that in order to conduct a successful campaign along the lines he had carefully planned, he would first have to beat Mackenzie to the field of action.

The objective, at least in Miles' view, was not merely to wipe out as many of the rebellious Indians as possible (as had always been Mackenzie's ambition). It was rather, first, to defeat them militarily; second, and equally important, to persuade them to take all their people back to the reservation; and to work out adequate and humane means to enable them to maintain a decent living standard there.

On August 10, Miles and his force departed from Fort Dodge. First objective was Adobe Walls, the buffalo hunters' camp some 150 miles south, far out on the bleak Staked Plains. The country was a scorching desert in summer, and in winter it could become a subzero blizzard-lashed wasteland.

There was no sure way of closely estimating the numerical strength of the Kiowa-Comanche war parties then outside the reservations. More important, there was no way of knowing whether such a large band as the one that had attacked Adobe Walls—reported to be several hundred strong—would remain intact or split up into small groups and scatter widely. Miles and his scouts (including such experts as Billy Dixon and Bat Masterson) knew the Indians could easily observe the strength of the Army force if it moved out as a unified command, in one body. The hostiles would then amass at least an equal number of braves and wait until the Army columns reached some spot best suited for an ambush. In such a situation, even if the Army forces should be able to defend themselves, they could not hope to do any great damage to the Indians.

A plan was worked out to confuse the Indians as to the

strength and movements of the Army units. If the Indians doubted they had a numerical advantage, they would probably divide and retreat southward, and thus be pursued effectively. To this end, Miles sent his most trusted officer, young Lt. Frank Baldwin, with a relatively small force, directly toward Adobe Walls. Meanwhile he took his main force, more than 700 men, along a different route some hundred miles farther east, through rugged and almost waterless desert country. The strategy was successful: the Indians divided their own forces to try to discover how many Army units were pursuing them, and they doubtless overestimated the Army's strength.

By the time Miles and Baldwin had rejoined on the Canadian River, a couple of weeks later, the Indians were retreating steadily southward and seemed to have lost their offensive assurance. From here on, Miles felt, his chief problem would be lack of supplies. Miles' immediate superior, General John Pope, who remained in his headquarters at Leavenworth, some 500 miles from the scene of action, had been ordered to send out supplies for 1,000 men, with reserves to last at least a month. The wagon trains arrived late and with only about a fourth as many wagons as had been specified.

Apparently Pope had trusted a supply officer named Van Vleit, and made no effort to check on his activities. Miles, in one of his frequent letters to Mary, told her he was sure Van Vleit was in cahoots with the supply contractors and was probably lining his own pockets with a good share of the funds. He also sent indignant and outspoken reports to Pope, who proceeded to ignore them. The troops were often on short rations, and the cavalry horses starved to death in some cases. The whole command was forced to wait out weeks, and once had to march back a hundred miles to meet a supply train, when they could otherwise have been in action.

All the many accounts of this campaign—official reports, letters, journals, and historical pieces—add up to a tale of hardships about as severe as anything to be found in the annals of the Old West. Less than a month after departing with high hopes from Fort Dodge, Miles was so plagued with troubles there were nights when he never got to sleep. The supply shortage continued, and it was so persistently ignored by Pope and the higher levels of command that Miles began to believe it was a deliberate move to keep him from advancing very far down into the Indian country. He knew Pope did not like him and was jealous of his reputation for fearlessness and ability in action. (Pope himself had emerged from the Civil War with quite a different sort of reputation.)

Major Price, meanwhile, had come to the aid of a wagon train that was being badly harassed by Indian raiders. It was an action which improved Price's position in that he was now supported by the wagon train's escort of troopers and scouts. But a little later he refused to rescue some ambushed scouts who, by his inaction, lost a couple of men. Miles was sure Price could not be relied upon to lead his men into action if a sharp fight were anticipated, a prediction that was later borne out. As for Davidson, he had allowed numerous Indians to escape in his rear and made no effort to contain them.

Though Miles had been successful in driving the Indians south, he feared they might well run into Mackenzie's forces before he could catch up with them, and Mackenzie would get the credit for their final defeat. In that event, if anyone were to be promoted for service in the Kiowa-Comanche campaign, it would be Mackenzie. The prospect was especially galling to Miles because for three or four years, while he had been kept on post duty at Leavenworth, his rival had been given ample chance to clear up the Indian situation in Texas. Instead Mackenzie, though often getting his name in the headlines, had only made matters worse and was, in Miles' opinion, largely responsible for the Indians' final all-out war against the whites.

But the high command didn't see it that way. Thinking in

47

the upper echelons still followed the popular line, indeed an almost universal line at the time on the part of the press, the public, and the government. It was, in brief, the concept that all so-called "fighting tribes"—such as the Sioux, Apaches, and Cheyennes, or Kiowas and Comanches—were "red devils" and "varmints," subhuman, torturers of women and children, capable of endless treachery, etc., etc. So they should be dealt with in kind—show them no quarter, kill all their wounded, beat and starve their women and children into submission. Miles was disgusted when Baldwin reported that the buffalo hunters at Adobe Walls, after the fight, had gone out and chopped off the heads of all the dead Indians and stuck them up on poles around the fort.

An incident of the Kiowa-Comanche campaign that was featured in newpapers throughout the country, over a period of months, was the Germaine affair. When the outbreak began, a Cheyenne raiding party swung up into Kansas and killed a settler named Germaine, his wife, and two grown children. Four younger children, all girls and the youngest only seven, had apparently been carried away by the Indians. A problem of the greatest concern to Miles was the rescue of these children. If they were still alive, he was determined to find a way of persuading their captors to give them up, without making some false move along the way which would induce the Indians to kill them.

So great was the dramatic appeal of the story of the Germaine sisters that various versions continued to appear for 25 years afterward. One account, in the quaint prose of its time, imagines the plight of the captured girls as follows:

It is almost impossible to describe the fate to which these children were doomed among the uncouth savages. The life they had to endure, the tortures to which they were subjected, are too revolting to recite. Their innocence and tender age offered no protection from the outrages of their captors; their prayers

48

and tears failed to move the hearts of their fiendish tormentors. They were looked upon by the males as common property and by the squaws as objects of pleasure and pastime for their consorts. . . . With sullen resignation the sisters prepared themselves to die among the savages, far away from their friends and white people.

The first decisive battle of the campaign began on the morning of August 30, in a scorched wasteland about 100 miles south of the Canadian River. Baldwin was scouting about a mile or two ahead of the main force, with a few troopers and some Delaware Indians. They were attacked by a large band of hostiles, in a rough stretch of country, while crossing a dry creek bed.

At sound of the shooting, Miles ordered up all his units on the double, sending out flanking detachments of cavalry as they advanced. They found Baldwin holding in good shape, and the Indians were soon dispersed. But this phase of the battle was the easiest, and Miles knew it was only an apparent victory. The enemy must not be allowed to break off contact; they must be pursued and harassed as they went if they were to be hurt at all seriously. Miles' study of Indian warfare had convinced him it was the lack of this technique which had made so many of the Army actions in the West ineffectual. All that day the troops pushed hard, in a killing heat of up to 110 degrees, with water supplies exhausted. But by nightfall many bands of Indians had been overtaken and routed; a substantial number of them were killed, and they had suffered a severe loss of supplies and arms.

Miles would have liked to have kept up his aggressive pursuit until all the belligerent Indians had been killed, captured, or driven back into the reservations. Because of the lack of supplies, he had to turn back after a few days. The delayed wagon train made it necessary for his whole force to march back 140 miles to meet it. Worst of all, on reaching his base on the Washita River, he found a dispatch from headquarters telling him that from here on, he would have to fetch his own supplies with his own wagons.

Nelson Miles was already quite well known in military circles for possessing a temper of the same larger-than-life proportions as his huge frame and boundless energy. But it was a temper always, so far as is recorded, under complete and icy control; probably he would have preferred the term "righteous indignation." In any case, when aroused he never failed to make his feelings sharply clear, even in the most official reports and dispatches. And if some of these missives might well get passed along to the desk of the general of the Army, or even the President, and the blunt honesty of a mere colonel be received as nothing less than sheer arrogance, it was all right with Miles. For all his ambition, if his promotion were to depend on bootlicking or any other form of currying favor from superiors, Miles was quite likely to remain a colonel forever, and not a very popular one at that.

In the case of the delayed wagon trains and reduced supplies, Miles kept up a steady flow of dispatches to General Pope, along the following lines: If properly supplied, he could have ended the Kiowa-Comanche campaign in a matter of weeks after the first decisive victory below the Canadian River. He knew that Custer, on a similar march with the same number of men a year earlier, had been allotted 400 supply wagons; so why had he, Miles, been allotted only 200? How did Pope think he could direct field operations from 500 miles away, when it took up to two weeks to put through an order? Why was nobody checking on the delinquencies of Van Vleit, the supply officer? And so on.

Pope was, quite naturally, infuriated. But it appears he didn't quite dare to recall Miles. In his letters to Mary, Miles said he thought Pope might be deliberately trying to prevent his command from rendering more effective action, to deprive it of credit for the Indians' most severe defeat of the campaign, which it had already accomplished, and that Pope was hoping the ultimate credit would go mostly to Mackenzie and the others.

He also wrote Mary that her uncle, General Sherman, seemed to have a singular lack of information as to what was going on. It is somewhat difficult, at this distance in time, to assess how accurate Miles' assumptions in this may have been. But the records would seem to show that in the remainder of the Kiowa-Comanche campaign, he was certainly getting a minimum of either credit or physical support from his superiors. If Pope really hoped to hold him back to a secondary position in the remaining operations, it was a futile hope. Miles was going to keep up his offensive action, so long as he could outride and outthirst and outwork the toughest man in his command. There were times when the whole outfit subsisted on small game and an occasional "buffler," but they stuck it out.

The campaign dragged along toward winter. From a start with troopers collapsing from heat and nearly dying of thirst (all the old reports mention men "cutting their own veins to obtain moisture"), the men now began to suffer from the cold. Before long they would be marching and fighting and camping in zero blizzards.

The high spot of the autumn, for Miles, was the rescue of the two younger Germaine children. While encamped at his supply base on the Washita, early in November, he had sent out a reconnoitering column under his right-hand man, Baldwin. The column surprised an encampment of Indians and completely routed them. The braves scattered in a hurry, leaving all their tepees and most of their supplies. In one of the tepees the troopers found the little girls, aged seven and nine. They were nearly starved but not harmed otherwise. Miles sent the children up to Leavenworth, where Mary made arrangements for their care and rehabilitation.

There were still many hostiles roaming around the region.

Mackenzie, Davidson, and Price had not accomplished much with their respective commands, it would seem, except to drive more Indians into Miles' territory. For a time there were many sharp attacks on the wagon trains, and a few men were killed and several wounded.

Major Price was ordered (from headquarters) to remain with the Miles command and act as a permanent escort for the wagons along the supply line. In one of the most active engagements Miles had with the hostiles, Price was near enough to hear the shooting, a mile or so distant. Miles found out afterward that Price, instead of hurrying to the scene, turned his men around and marched in the opposite direction. This resulted in a large band of Indians making a clean escape, when many could have been trapped if Price had come up.

With characteristic disregard for the fact that Price was a favorite of Pope and enjoyed the confidence of the higher echelons, Miles relieved the major of his command and sent him back north under arrest, together with serious charges against him all signed and sealed and properly attested by "Col. Nelson A. Miles, (brevet Maj. Gen.) Commanding." I have so far not been able to trace what happened to Price after he was delivered to headquarters. Very possibly nothing. Miles himself makes no further mention of the matter. But he had at least seen to it that Price would not bother him any more on this particular campaign.

With the approach of winter, Miles received orders to make a more or less permanent encampment and confine his movements entirely to "scouting expeditions." This had been the accepted winter routine of the Army for years, but it infuriated Miles, because he thought it was needlessly giving the Indians every advantage. They could feel quite safe throughout the winter months, regrouping and supplying themselves, and be ready to go on the warpath again in the spring.

Furthermore Miles felt that no letup in pushing the Indians should be tolerated so long as it was known they still held the older two Germaine sisters. Indian scouts had found that the girls were still alive and being held by a chief called Stone Calf, and Miles had hired a friendly Indian to contact them and deliver a letter telling them to keep up hope; in the letter he had enclosed a photograph Mary had sent him of their rescued younger sisters.

It was Miles' plan to ostensibly comply with the order to carry out only winter "scouting," but, in fact, to make his so-called scouting parties nothing less than a continued series of all-out attacks and pursuits of whatever Indians he could find, leading his men in person. To that end, he managed to equip his troops for winter warfare, even for subzero operations. Mary was of considerable help in this, being well aware of the situation. She saw to it that as much winter gear as could be found was sent out in the supply trains, including a gallon of old rye whiskey for use in severe emergencies, well disguised in case some teamster might decide to "lose" it in transit.

On December 2, from "Camp on the Washita," Miles wrote the following to Mary:

I am quietly waiting here for supplies, and as soon as they are received, I intend to make one more movement towards the head of Red River, with a hope of driving out the Indians that have taken refuge in that region or of making it uncomfortable for them, even if I cannot capture them. And possibly we may be able to do something towards rescuing those poor white girls who are still in their hands. As much as I long to return to my darling little family, I am unwilling to turn eastward and leave them in captivity. Last night I could not sleep thinking about their sufferings. I judge from the story told by the younger ones that a scene is enacted in their camp every night that would chill the blood of the sternest soldier in my command. . . .

He went on to tell how his men had almost starved because of Van Vleit, the supply officer he suspected of graft. Van Vleit had been ordered to confer with him at his encampment but hadn't appeared, sending word from a Kansas outpost that he was "too sick" to proceed any farther at that time. Miles implied to Mary that if Van Vleit ever put in an appearance he would soon have reason to feel a lot sicker than he claimed to be.

Miles wrote again a couple of weeks later:

> Camp at the Head of White Deer Creek,
> South of Adobe Walls
> Dec. 17, 1874
>
> . . . After remaining nearly a month in that most disagreeable camp, waiting for supplies, I left on the 14th, marched out on the plains, and camped near a waterhole. The next day marched in a snow storm to Red Deer Creek, cleared away the snow, pitched our tents, and the next day marched to this point. I intend to go to the head of Munster Creek and then may strike down the head of Red River, if I do not get information to take me elsewhere. I have with me only one company of cavalry but shall take other troops as circumstances require. My men are in good spirits and fairly provided for the winter climate. I have sent back all but three companies of cavalry and three companies of infantry of the original command, and shall start the 8th cavalry [back] to New Mexico as soon as the Keokuk contractors furnish grain. I am bound to make one effort to drive in what Indians remain out [of the reservations] and rescue if possible those little girls. I know the chief who has one or both of them. He offered to trade them to some Mexicans for squaws. I expect my command will be withdrawn [by orders from Division Headquarters] even when it is in a position to finish this affair, and against my earnest protest. Yet any man who gives the order to withdraw troops under these circumstances and leaves those innocent sufferers to their fate, damns his name to eternal infamy. . . . It does seem as if the General of the Army could afford to take a little time and interest in this important matter. There never was a campaign more grossly mismanaged.

Poor Mary. She wanted to be loyal to her Uncle Cump, most illustrious general in the U.S. Army and its present top commander, but her husband often wrote about him in terms rather far from flattering. If any of those letters should ever happen to reach eyes other than hers, Miles might get a quick discharge rather than a quick promotion.

It was a rough winter for the troops remaining in the field. There were a few cases of frozen feet, and Miles himself got a frosted ear while riding out in a blizzard. But the "scouting" paid off. Constantly kept on the run, Chief Stone Calf, leader of the largest band of hostiles still out, agreed to surrender in February. Miles' terms called for the safe return of the older Germaine sisters, seventeen and fifteen, who were released, terribly ragged and thin but in quite good health. The Kiowas and Comanches and their Cheyenne allies, starved, half-frozen, and discouraged, either surrendered to the troops or returned to their reservations and gave up their arms. They would never fight again.

Pope apparently decided it would be expedient to forget his heated exchanges with Miles. His official reports, while not giving Miles any personal credit that could possibly be omitted, state that the whole campaign was an unqualified success and clearly indicate that Miles' command must have been largely responsible.

Miles was, as usual, well satisfied with his own conduct in the campaign. And if he had made a few rather powerful enemies by his independent action and his outspoken and sometimes vituperative dispatches, he was not likely to lose any sleep over it. He returned to Leavenworth in high spirits and settled down for a well-earned rest with his family. Though still quite desperately poor at the time, it apparently never occurred to him that the Germaine sisters were no longer his personal responsibility, and that their care might be left to others. He had himself appointed their guardian and remained such until all four had grown up and married.

6

THE next major Indian campaign after the Kiowa-Comanche hostiles had been subdued began the following year, 1876. All during 1875 various subdivisions of the Sioux nation had been leaving their reservations and preparing for war against the invading whites. The country involved was so vast, roughly 1,000 miles east-west by 500 north-south (now comprising Nebraska, the Dakotas, Wyoming, Montana, Idaho), and some of it so little known, there were certain wild bands of Sioux who had never been herded into any reservation at all. Others had been assigned to one reservation after another, only to have ranchers, miners, or buffalo hunters arrive to push them on again into less productive lands. Nobody, least of all the Army high command and the Indian affairs officials in Washington, had the slightest idea what the total Sioux population was at the time, nor were there any estimates of how many armed hostiles might be at large.

Meanwhile, Grant's Secretary of War, William Belknap, and an Indian agent were caught red-handed in a scheme to line their own pockets with the funds allotted to protect and support the Oklahoma Indian territory. Absorbed as he was in such pressing affairs of state as trying to explain what had happened to the cash that never arrived at the Indian territory, the Secretary of War left the direction of the Army entirely to Sherman. The autocratic Sherman, dedicated to his chain-of-command system, in turn delegated to Sheridan almost complete authority for running his Division of the Missouri, and hence the conduct of the Sioux campaign.

Sheridan was a seasoned Indian fighter, but in totally different terrain and against tribes far less organized and less skillful than the Sioux. He was of no mind to assume direct personal responsibility for what might happen next; and he continued the passing along of authority down the line to his field officers, especially to generals George Crook and Alfred Terry. Smaller units under various colonels, Custer, Mackenzie, Gibbon, and others, were often far afield, also entirely on their own, for long periods.

The whole setup, as Miles saw it from his post at Leavenworth, made less than no sense at all. There was no unified or integrated command and no common stated policy on how to deal with the Indians. Each commander went his own way, often completely ignorant of where the others were operating and with little exchange of information. Worse still, Miles suspected certain commanders were mainly interested in finding only such small Indian forces as they could defeat without being supported, and thereby be able to claim victories for themselves. By the same token, they would avoid contact with any known hostile force large enough to denote a real threat, necessitating aid from a rival commander.

Miles bombarded Sherman with personal letters expressing these views in very blunt language. He hoped that Sherman would see what was going on and promote him to a position where he could improve the situation and perhaps avoid impending war with the Sioux. The letters seemed to have an opposite effect on the general of the Army; and, had not Miles been married to Sherman's favorite niece, he would probably have been sacked for telling the commander-in-chief how to run the Army. Uncle Cump showed no delight when Miles informed him in detail how his general officers were failing to lick the Indian problem—Crook independent and vain, Terry ignorant of geography and Indian psychology, Sheridan always so far away he received information weeks too late to give intelligent orders, etc.

Miles had sent East for every book that could be found about Indian history, culture, and habitat. He was fascinated by the great differences of behavior, in ethnic terms, among the tribes, and he was rapidly becoming an authority on Indians generally, taking the trouble whenever he could to get to know them personally. But this was not a popular approach for an Army man of those days, and Miles might never have been allowed to get into the Sioux fighting at all except for the sudden and totally unexpected demise of his friend Custer.

It took about a month for news of the massacre to reach the outside world. When the steamer *Far West* landed at Bismarck, then the railhead, on July 5, she was carrying the wounded from Custer's surviving companies of the 7th Cavalry, after a trip of some 700 miles from the Big Horn River. From Bismarck the story was flashed by telegraph—Custer with five companies, somehow separated from the rest of his command, annihilated to the last man. The impact on the country at large was almost as shocking as another Sumter, or the future sinking of the *Maine*. There would be other savage Indian wars in the years ahead, but never another incident to compare with Custer's Last Stand. And so the Sioux campaign would forever afterward be a favorite subject of historians, bards, and scriptwriters.

Newspapers and magazines, that summer of 1876, offered all sorts of accounts of the massacre. The stories had one thing in common—they were wildly inaccurate. Custer was usually presented as a superhero, but of course there were those who took an opposite view and found him guilty of every kind of military error. (A difference of opinion that has lasted a century, as evidenced by frequent television Westerns in which Custer is variously depicted as anything from a fearless genius to a conceited dolt; likewise the Sioux, depending on the "angle," may appear as noble savages fighting to protect their women and children, or a pack of hideous fiends and torturers.)

Longfellow, more popular in his day than any half-dozen modern poets in ours, got busy right away. His epic, "The Revenge of Rain-in-the-Face," ends:

> But the foemen fled in the night,
> And Rain-in-the-Face, in his flight,
>   Uplifted high in air
> As a ghastly trophy, bore
> The brave heart, that beat no more,
> Of the White Chief with yellow hair.
> Whose was the right and the wrong,
> Sing it, O funeral song,
> With a voice that is full of tears,
> And say that our broken faith
> Wrought all this ruin and scathe,
>   In the Year of a Hundred Years.

Longfellow's thinking was better than his poetry. He was far ahead of the Congress and the Army in recognizing "our broken faith" as the sole cause of the Sioux war. But as for Custer's heart, Miles verified a couple of years later that it had not been molested; Custer had been killed instantly by two or three rifle slugs. No scalping.

Miles was more shaken and upset by Custer's defeat than he had been before in his whole career. He simply couldn't understand, he kept telling his wife, how an officer as able as Custer could have got himself into such a situation. It was known that Custer had divided his command into three columns and only the 300 men of the five companies he was leading himself were wiped out—the other two columns, totaling seven companies, under Major Reno and Captain Benteen, hadn't suffered heavily. Yet they must have been near enough, from their own accounts, to have gone to Custer's aid. There must have been some terrible error either in the planning or in the execution of the fight. Miles determined that at some future time he would make a careful check of the battle scene himself and get all the facts.

The immediate reaction of the War Department to the news of the massacre was to start an all-out push against the Sioux, and especially the hostiles under Sitting Bull. All available troops were ordered to the northern Wyoming-Montana area, where the Sioux, it was feared, might soon escape northward across the Canadian border. If this should happen, the military situation would become an impossible one. Several thousand Sioux, safe above the border, would be free to strike down into almost any place in the whole Northwest whenever they chose.

Even at this urgent juncture, neither Sheridan nor Sherman would order Miles out with a field command. They placed their faith in such commanders as their old favorites, Crook and Terry, who had botched this whole Sioux business so hopelessly for the past year and created a climate that led to the Custer massacre. They also brought up all their other trusted officers such as Mackenzie and Gibbon and Hazen, who knew nothing of the character of the country or Sioux tactics.

Though Miles' superiors showed no interest in sending him into action against the Sioux, they wanted to make full use of the junior officers and men he had so thoroughly trained and disciplined. He was ordered to send more than half of his command to Montana at once. It seems to have been assumed that he himself would remain at Leavenworth until he might be specifically ordered elsewhere. But Miles knew of an old military regulation which allowed the colonel of a regiment to lead the larger portion in person if his command were divided, no orders to the contrary being received. And so without waiting for further orders, Miles promptly embarked with his men on the 1,700-mile trip to the headwaters of the Yellowstone

River in the heart of the Sioux country. From Yankton, just across the river from the northern edge of Nebraska, the only transport was by riverboat; along the Missouri all the way up across the Dakotas, then west into Montana along the Yellowstone.

Miles' burning impatience to get into the field wherever there was likely to be some fighting must be seen in the context of his time. Warfare had not then become so civilized that only the young junior officers were sent out to the front lines, the positions of greatest danger. It was a few years later, in the Spanish-American War, that our generals first discovered it was much more comfortable to direct a distant army from their Washington offices, and more advantageous, whenever things went wrong, for the high command in Washington to blame mistakes on the officers in the field.

But Miles' education never reached this point. Though an innovator in many respects, he was a lifelong and fanatical believer in the theory that only the man on the scene can know best how to direct the action. In this he was supported during the Indian campaigns by the fact that communications from a field command to headquarters might take weeks, and sometimes a courier would not show up at all, his bleached bones possibly being found years later.

All accounts of the start of the Sioux campaign add up to what must have been one of the most ill-planned and unorganized military ventures in history. General Terry was in the field with a force of some 1,000 men, establishing various posts and supply lines along tributaries of the Yellowstone in the best West Point manner. No Sioux were ever likely to come within a hundred miles of any spot Terry had selected as suitable for giving them a fight. General Crook was more aggressive. But with little or no understanding of Sioux tactics, he was wandering more or less aimlessly with a massive and well-equipped force of 1,500 men, following weeks-old Indian tracks and making no effective use of scouts or intelligence. Sheridan's only plan was that somehow the Sioux could be caught between these two main forces.

The Sioux had plenty of scouts of their own, and as Miles had foreseen, they had no trouble avoiding the main Army forces in a territory a thousand miles wide. Whenever the Sioux did attack, they selected smaller detached units under Mackenzie, Gibbon, Hazen, and others. From such skirmishes they could often capture horses and supplies, hitting and running with little damage to themselves.

Miles himself had a command of some 500 men, but some had to be left in charge of base camps and supplies. His effective marching force was about 400 troops plus a few scouts and friendly Indians. Yet he wrote Mary, in all seriousness, that with this small force he hoped to get ahead of both Crook and Terry, catch up with Sitting Bull, and give the Sioux a decisive defeat. It was now known that the Sioux, if they chose to band together to any great extent, could rally a force of warriors numbering into the thousands. Thus we should perhaps have some sympathy for the position taken by Sheridan and Sherman. They must truly have thought Miles was rash, if not mad, especially in light of what had happened to Custer. They never understood how very much more Miles knew about Indians and Indian tactics than had his more theatrical late fellow colonel.

Throughout the fall the Sioux continued to maintain every advantage. They were among the world's best horsemen, and on their home ground could easily outdistance the Army forces. But Miles' studies of the situation convinced him that in winter the Indians would become vulnerable. Also they would not be prepared to go on fighting, expecting that the Army, as in the past, would avoid winter action for the most part.

Terry, nominally commanding combined operations under Sheridan, refused to believe that effective winter campaigning could be carried out in this country where temperatures sometimes dropped to 60 below zero. His plans called for general withdrawal in late fall; such forces as were left in Montana would be settled in permanent log-house cantonments until spring. Only such scouting would be continued as seemed necessary to protect these cantonments from attack. Miles was hugely disgusted with this whole approach. Somewhat as he had done in the Kiowa-Comanche affair, he planned to make his own scouting a full-scale offensive, using all the men in his command. He hoped to keep the Sioux on the move and to continuously harass them in every way possible.

Miles' confidence was based in part on his knowledge that in severe winter weather the Indians would have to separate into smaller bands, scattering widely, in order to find enough game and other food to survive. Only in warmer months could they keep a large force of warriors together, such as that which proved too much for Custer—two or three thousand braves in one encampment.

Much valuable information, Miles knew, could be learned from paying attention to such expert scouts as Bill Cody and Yellowstone Kelley. Miles also believed that the Army could devise winter clothing superior to that worn by the Indians, enabling troops to travel in cold at least as severe as the savages could withstand. To this end he put every man in his command, as soon as the cantonment huts were built, to making Arctic-style outfits. Underwear was sewn from blankets; hoods, coats, and robes were made from buffalo hides; outer boots were improvised to insulate the footwear. And so it seems that the credit must go to Miles for being the first Army man to design and test out workable Arctic equipment, an innovation more than sixty years in advance of the official Arctic gear developed in World War II.

Miles was not very optimistic about getting much support from the commands of Crook and Terry. In his letters to Mary throughout the campaign, various remarks showed quite clearly what he thought of the popular Crook, who had been given the generalship Miles was still trying vainly to obtain. Though Crook's command had been badly defeated in a battle with the Sioux a few days before the Custer massacre, Sheridan and Sherman still placed great faith in him. At least Crook did not urge treating the Indians as though they were an honorable enemy who might be brought around eventually to a surrender through negotiating, as the upstart Colonel Miles kept insisting in his reports.

On July 19 Miles wrote Mary a letter describing the exciting and scenically magnificent boat trip up the Yellowstone and telling her he hoped to get in touch with the troops of either Terry or Crook, referring to the latter with the comment: "I understand General Crook was getting ready to move (he has been doing that for a year) on Aug. 1st. . . ."

And again, on August 2: "From all I can learn from the officers, General Crook makes no comments nor gives General Terry any information. . . ."

On August 4, writing of needless delays of the riverboat because of a lack of cooperation from Crook: "No one here knows where Crook is, *or* the Indians. . . . It is expected we will move up the Rosebud and find the Indians or find Crook. . . . I shall be happily surprised if the thing is not a dead failure and the result is the lasting disgrace of the army."

On August 20: "On the tenth we met Crook's command making one of his magnificent scouts, as senseless and ill-advised as it was fruitless. After a month of delay and preparation he leaves . . . with fifteen days' supplies. We met him, or he joined us, with his animals nearly exhausted on a trail fifteen days old, according to some scouts . . . but anyway so old that he had not the remotest chance of catching the Indians. Had he not got some supplies from my command he would have been compelled to travel back on his own trail at the end of the seventh day."

On February 5: "I am surprised to learn that he turned his

back on a very large Indian camp; it must have been within forty miles of his camp, and had been there for weeks. I think his official report is the most extraordinary document ever signed by a Brigadier General. . . ."

And near the end of the campaign, on March 15: "I would be very glad if Crook would explain why he turned around, marched the other way and remained in camp fourteen days when the Crow scouts offered to take him to Crazy Horse's camp in six days. The fact is, he scarcely thought it possible for me to reach Crazy Horse's camp at all with my poor mules. . . ."

Finally, when the Indians were surrendering, he wrote Mary on March 17: "I presume if they go south, Crook will go out to meet them and claim the credit for bagging them. Yet he has had no more to do with it than if he had been in Egypt. . . ."

Miles was only a shade more polite in his official reports whenever referring to Crook's movements. He had written Sherman a letter stating that if he, Miles, were given command of the campaign, he could quickly bring the Sioux to terms with a force of not more than fifteen hundred troops. Sherman of course ignored this, but left Miles more or less free to follow his own course with the 450 men in his personal command.

As for General Terry, Miles had a high regard for him personally but felt that his command was accomplishing even less than Crook's against the Sioux. Meanwhile a third general, Hazen, had been sent to the scene with another large command. But Hazen, like Terry, didn't believe in winter operations and planned merely to hold his men in winter quarters until spring.

7

THAT winter there were three generals in the field, each
with a force of some 1,500 well-equipped men, operating
independently of each other. The only plan they had in common was that none would take any real action during the
winter months. There were also the colonels Mackenzie and
Gibbon, who were more or less independent. Mackenzie's con-
tribution to the campaign, in late fall, was to attack a small
village of Cheyennes, allies of the Sioux, and massacre all the
women and children and such braves as hadn't escaped. For
this Mackenzie was hailed as a hero in Washington, and the
Eastern papers played up the act as an important victory of the
Sioux campaign. And lastly there was Miles, with his small
force, outranked by the three generals and less favored by the
high command than the other colonels. Yet Miles alone was
preparing to continue active fighting throughout the winter.

This almost unbelievable situation seems to have come
about largely because Sheridan never exactly defined which of
the three generals, Crook, Terry, or Hazen, was to be Miles'
immediate superior, and none of the three was at all anxious to
assume this responsibility. They had all, at one time or another,
felt the sting of Miles' outspoken reports, and they knew of his
habit of writing personal letters to his wife's uncle, General
Sherman. For his own part, Miles bypassed the three generals
as far as he could, reporting whenever possible directly to the

headquarters command. And in this manner he went ahead with his plans to keep up a series of winter forays against the Sioux.

Actually Miles had much more in mind than just attacking the Sioux effectively. He wanted to persuade them to surrender *before* a general war of extermination would be necessary. Such a war would result in great losses to the Army as well as to the Indians, he felt sure. There would probably be more affairs like the Custer massacre. If the Sioux were allowed to rest throughout the winter and regroup in the spring, they would be ready to resume the war with even greater determination than they had shown the previous year. But if they could be dealt a decisive blow in winter, they might see the ultimate hopelessness of keeping up the fight.

In December and early January, there were heavy snows and temperatures down to 30 below zero. Miles led his men out on extended scouting expeditions, which proved satisfactory. The command then went into action. Scouts located the scattered winter camps of the Sioux, and these were attacked and routed, one by one. The Sioux began to try to rally and consolidate against these unexpected actions. On January 8, at Wolf Mountain, they thought they had gathered a sufficient force of mounted warriors to defeat anything Miles could send against them. Miles figured he was outnumbered about three to one but felt confident that his superior equipment and organization, plus the use of two small field pieces he had brought along, would justify taking a stand. And he chose a position in partly wooded, rough country where the Indians could not charge effectively on horseback.

The main fighting, in a subzero snowstorm, lasted some eight hours. The Indians, led by one of their most able chiefs, Crazy Horse, attacked in force several times, but recklessly and for the most part on foot, a form of fighting they were unaccustomed to. Their losses were heavy, while the soldiers lost only two or three men and several wounded. At the end the

Sioux retreated in a disorganized rout, pursued aggressively by the forward line of troops until it was certain they would not attempt any resumption of the fight.

Though it was not known at the time, this proved to be the decisive battle of the whole campaign. There were many other skirmishes during the next two or three months, but these were mainly efforts by the Sioux to capture supplies. They were approaching starvation in many of their camps, and the women and children were beginning to come in to the Army posts.

Meanwhile Miles' idea of parleys with the chiefs had been carried out with some success. Even the great Sitting Bull had met with Miles, at one point, under a flag of truce. The wily old Sioux leader would not give in to the government terms for a cease-fire—surrender of all arms and ammunition and a return to the reservations where his people had been starving; in short, no real assurance that his people would be any better off than they had before the fighting began. Miles could only promise to try his best to persuade the government to give the Sioux a fairer deal, but this wasn't enough.

There were many, in the Army and outside, who thought Miles should have nabbed Sitting Bull when he had the chance—Redskins were murderers and should be caught by any means possible. Miles was openly contemptuous of such criticism. Ethics aside, he was sure that making a martyr of Sitting Bull would only provoke the Sioux to go on fighting to the last man. He knew that officers had been killed under flags of truce by treacherous Indians and that every time he went out to parley there might be a bullet waiting for him. Once a young brave got excited and did take a shot at him, but Miles had seen him raise his rifle and wheeled his horse in time to avoid getting hit; the slug killed one of the six soldiers in Miles' escort.

Eventually the old Sioux chief retreated with a small band of followers into Canada. But after Wolf Mountain his power was broken, and by far the greater part of the Sioux tribes and their Cheyenne allies decided to give up and surrender their arms. Throughout April and May most of the hostiles still out, some five thousand in all, turned themselves in at Army posts and reservations. The critical period of the Sioux campaign was over. The rest would be only minor mopping-up operations.

Historians, having read innumerable books about the Sioux campaign and having studied the War Department records of all the commands involved, down to the last detail, will doubtless feel that I have accorded Miles too much credit. Perhaps so. But I will rest my case on the final official reports of the two men, Sheridan and Sherman, who had all along been counting on generals Crook, Terry, and Hazen, rather than young Colonel Miles, with his ridiculously meager force on "scouting operations," to defeat the Sioux.

Sherman's report is dated July 17, 1877:

> I now regard the Sioux Indian problem, as a war question, as solved by the operations of General Miles last winter and by the establishment of the two new posts on the Yellowstone, now assured this summer. Boats come and go now, where a year ago none would venture except with strong guards. Wood-yards are being established to facilitate navigation, and the great mass of the hostiles have been forced to go to the agencies for food and protection, or have fled across the border to the British territory.

Sheridan's report, October 25, 1877:

> During the months of December and January the hostile Indians were constantly harassed by the troops under Col. Nelson A. Miles, Fifth Infantry, whose headquarters were at the mouth of the Tongue River, and who had two sharp engagements with them, inflicting heavy losses in men, supplies, and animals.
> This constant pounding and ceaseless activity upon the part of our troops (Colonel Miles in particular) in midwinter began

to tell, and early in February, 1877, information was communicated which led me to believe that the Indians in general were tired of the war, and that the large bodies heretofore in the field were beginning to break up.

In the mean time Colonel Miles, having had information of the whereabouts of Lame Deer's band of hostile Sioux, surprised his camp, killing 14 warriors, including Lame Deer and Iron Star, the two principal chiefs, capturing 450 ponies, and destroying 51 lodges and their contents. This band commenced to surrender, in small squads of from two to twenty, immediately thereafter, until at length, on the 10th of September, the last of the band, numbering 224, constantly followed and pressed by troops from the command of Colonel Miles, surrendered at Camp Sheridan.

A small detail in Sherman's report caught my eye: the use of "General Miles" in contrast to Sheridan's "Col. Nelson A. Miles." Could it be that the crusty old commander-in-chief's conscience was bothering him a little, and he used the colonel's former title of Civil War days as a courtesy, a sort of tacit appreciation of Miles' remarkable success in this campaign, even though Sherman was still not ready to try to get his nephew-in-law promoted to brigadier? In any case, almost four years went by before the long-sought promotion to brigadier general finally materialized. Probably no other officer in Army history had to work so hard or accomplish so much in order to achieve it. But in fairness to Sherman, it is a fact that during the quarter century after the Civil War, Congress never appropriated enough money to support more than a dozen or so general officers in the entire Army. To promote Miles, Sherman would have had to pass over many older and better-known men, West Pointers and former high-ranking Civil War officers, men who were often directly recommended by the Secretary of War or the President himself.

Perhaps Mary Miles, in her many letters over the years written on her husband's behalf (sometimes without telling him)

70

to General Sherman and her other uncle, the Ohio Senator, had been asking the impossible. Perhaps she wrote mainly to keep her husband from losing hope, and to show her own persistent and unlimited faith in his ability. In my own view, it would seem that Sherman might at least have made some gesture toward a promotion for Miles at the end of the Sioux campaign, on the basis of his own reports of the colonel's key role in the outcome.

But aside from his commitment to the seniority system, there were probably two other reasons for Sherman's continuing silence on the matter of a promotion. First, he was still touchy on the subject of nepotism, and more than once he wrote Miles angry instructions to desist from writing him personal letters concerning high military decisions instead of sending them up through the chain of command in the proper official manner. (Miles didn't pay the slightest attention to this.) Second, he himself had no real knowledge of Indians or the subtleties of Indian fighting; it would take even more than the Kiowa-Comanche and Sioux affairs to convince him of the enormous difference in ability between men like Custer or Crook and Nelson Miles.

As Sherman saw it, Custer had just been unlucky, while Miles—so far, at least—had been lucky. He may even have been influenced by the widely quoted but wholly unlikely theory (at first even considered by Miles) that Custer, on his last expedition, had inflicted such heavy losses on Sitting Bull's forces that the task of rounding them up had been made much easier. Actually, according to the later testimony of several chiefs, the Sioux had been so flushed with victory after the Custer fight that they felt they could defy the Army indefinitely. And in fact they did give Crook's large command a bad beating the second and last time he ever encountered any great number of them.

Longfellow wrote no poem about the Battle of Wolf Mountain. Quite possibly he never heard of it. And the ultimate fate of Sitting Bull has faded into an obscure corner of frontier history. I remember my surprise and excitement, when working on the Westminster town history, at discovering that Miles was the man who defeated Sitting Bull after the Custer massacre. And the defeat, I learned, had been accomplished in winter snows with not very many more men than Custer's five companies. (Custer's whole command, of course, had been much larger than Miles'; but he had separated his force at the wrong time, and the seven other companies under Reno and Benteen had not come up in time to save him.)

I'm reminded of a conversation with a young friend, an assistant professor of American history at Harvard who had just written a well-received book on certain aspects of nineteenth-century American history. In his extensive research, I was sure he must have read more about Miles than I then had. I made some remark to the effect that every schoolboy knows Sitting Bull got Custer, but nobody seems to know that it was Miles who finally got Sitting Bull.

"Oh, sure, Miles was the great Indian fighter," my historian friend replied. "Let's see, now—was this the General Miles who figured in the Civil War, or the one who took Puerto Rico in the Spanish-American War?" When I told him one and the same, he still seemed a little doubtful.

But though Miles had beaten the Sioux by the summer of 1877, he had still not been able to capture Sitting Bull and the hard-core band of warriors who escaped with him over the Canadian line. For this Miles blamed the higher echelon of command which had refused to assign any cavalry to support his small infantry force. He had written Sherman at the outset that if he could be allotted even one battalion of cavalry, he could cut off Sitting Bull's escape. He believed that so long as Sitting Bull was at large, the old renegade could become a rallying point for future Indian uprisings—which turned out to be quite evident a couple of months later, in the Nez Perce war.

Besides his experiments with Arctic equipment, the Sioux campaign gave Miles an idea for another innovation. By the end of winter, after Sitting Bull had got away to the north, Miles had become thoroughly tired of the difficulties of moving infantry on foot in a big country without transport. They had captured large numbers of Indian ponies and, on an impulse, Miles one morning ordered every man in his command to take a pony from the corral and learn to ride it.

The result, as he described it later with great relish, was for a while better than a three-ring circus, and there was more cursing than was ever heard on the battle-field. The ponies were pretty wild, and some of the men had little or no experience in this form of exercise. Often soldiers were tossed off several times before they got the hang of it, to the delight of the more expert. But anything was better than the endless foot-slogging, sometimes up to thirty miles a day, that the men had been enduring for months. Miles thus initiated what might be called the first organized "mounted infantry" in the U.S. Army. It would not be until World War II that the trend would be complete, and infantry units no longer moved over long distances by marching on foot.

In July, 1877, a number of Army wives made the long boat trip to the cantonment in Montana. When Mary Miles found that her husband would have to remain in the Montana country for perhaps another year, she decided to join him, taking seven-year-old Cecelia. Her unmarried sister, Elizabeth Sherman, also went along. It was a wild trip. Two steamers set out together, and partway upriver one of them hit a snag and sank. Mary and Elizabeth and Cecelia were on the unlucky boat. Everybody got off safely, but the women lost several trunks— most of what they had brought except the clothes they were wearing.

At the log-house cantonment, they found that Miles was off on an extended scouting expedition and not expected back for some days. There was an Indian encampment nearby, where hundreds of Sioux awaited a decision from the government as to where they were going to be permanently settled. Nightly powwows and occasional fights made the post a scene of constant excitement, and the two sisters were not too happy until Miles finally returned to welcome them.

Then, for a few weeks, Mary and Elizabeth, not to mention little Cecelia, had an outing that must have given them fantastic memories for the rest of their lives. Miles, an ebullient giant hard as a Sioux brave after his months of campaigning, couldn't wait to show the girls all the natural wonders of the wilderness he had discovered. Accompanied by an armed escort, they rode out on camping excursions into country no white woman had ever seen. Bands of friendly Crow Indians followed them just to observe what sort of creatures Mary and Elizabeth could be.

On one such trip, a scout came up to tell Miles a band of hostile Sioux, doubtless some stragglers following Sitting Bull northward, was camped just ahead. The women were rushed back to the cantonment and a column of troops sent out. Miles led a chase after the Sioux, caught up with them, and fought a sharp skirmish in which one or two soldiers and several Indians were killed. Afterward, Miles rode back to resume vacationing with his family, as unconcerned, it seemed to Mary, as though he had just been out rabbit shooting.

Sherman came up to inspect the new posts, and the Mileses put on as elaborate a reception as they could manage at their newly built, rather crude headquarters. The old general was for once almost openly enthusiastic at the efficiency Miles had shown in building and maintaining the post and the spit-and-polish deportment of the troops. The cantonment was called Fort Keogh, and the adjoining encampment of the surrendered Indians was nicknamed Miles City. (The name stuck, and present-day Miles City stands on the site.) During the summer Miles completed a four-room house, and Mary prepared to live there as long as her husband would be stationed at Keogh.

At about this point, Nelson A. Miles was becoming a familiar name in national newspapers. But, while his reputation as an Indian fighter began to be played up back East and in the country at large, he was also becoming a figure of some controversy. This controversy not only continued throughout his long life but left many echoes in everything that has been written about him, even to the present day.

In a rare moment of reflection, after the Sioux campaign, Miles wrote Mary that many of his fellow officers didn't seem to like him, and he couldn't understand why. The fact was, of course, they resented his relentless and aggressive pursuit of promotion. Some officers, when Miles defeated the Indians after they had failed, claimed that he exaggerated his victories to further his own ambitions.

If this were true, Miles certainly behaved most peculiarly after the Sioux had been rounded up. He incurred the disfavor of all his superiors, from Sheridan to the President, by demanding that the Sioux be treated humanely and allowed to return to the reservations they had been promised. All his pleas were ignored; the Sioux were split up and sent to agencies farther east, where many died of disease and malnutrition. Miles could hardly have thought that the kind of fight he put up on the Indians' behalf—a pattern that followed all his Indian campaigns—would help earn him a promotion. And there is plenty of evidence that if he had rested on his laurels as an Indian fighter, instead of also fighting politicians and others who were taking lands from the Indians and neglecting their rights, he would have been promoted much sooner.

Those same traits which caused Miles to be so disliked by some of his colleagues, and by all politicians, brought him certain friends and admirers. The sort of military men who are interested in performance and care nothing about the vagaries of public opinion—men like Hancock and Grant—had an ever stronger confidence in Miles. Grant, sometime after he was President, remarked that he considered Miles, though still a colonel, among the five ablest officers in the entire army.

8

IN the fall of 1877 the end of the Sioux campaign merged into the start of yet another bloody war, the revolt of the Nez Perce Indians who moved eastward into the same general area. Like the Sioux, the Nez Perce had decided to fight rather than starve, though it had often been said that the Nez Perce tribes had not killed a white man in a century. Heretofore their domain had been far enough west to be safe from invasion by many settlers; but now their lands had been overrun, and as usual, the government had backed the ranchers and miners who staked out claims in Indian reservations and hunting grounds.

Rather than go into any detail on this campaign of more than two months, in the course of which Miles became the decisive figure (much the same as in the Sioux campaign), it may be more pertinent here to discuss a very recent book, *The Flight of the Nez Perce: A History of the Nez Perce War,* by Col. Mark H. Brown. It is probably the most complete and thoroughly researched account of the Nez Perce campaign ever written. Some idea of the complexity of that Indian war is indicated just by the book's 35 solid pages of notes, bibliography, and acknowledgments, following its 431 pages of narrative. The author must have consulted just about everything ever written about his subject—some hundred books, countless newspapers and magazines, and voluminous War Department records and reports.

After such monumental research, I will accept the author's *factual* material pertaining to Miles: the large number of quotes from records, journals, etc., and Brown's own narration. But whenever Brown inserts, from time to time, his opinion of Miles' character—the kind of man he assumes Miles was, and what his motivations were in doing or saying this or that —I must disagree most sharply and totally. Here Brown has fallen into the same trap that caught many others. In some instances I feel quite sure I know, from my own researches, just what Brown read that led him to parrot a particular observation—for example, that Miles had been a "persistent offender" one year in the matter of giving the newspapers accounts that accorded him "more than his share of the glory."

The first half of Brown's book deals mostly with the immensely complicated background of the Nez Perce outbreak and the hundreds of characters involved, together with a vastly more detailed explanation of the Army chain-of-command system than I have given here. Miles is mentioned only briefly. (Somewhat grudgingly and obliquely, it is noted that he was the officer who finally defeated the Sioux.) But in the second half of the book, Miles becomes more and more prominent, and toward the end he has the full spotlight, in that he commands the troops which finally overcome the Nez Perce in the most important battle of the story. However, I got the distinct impression that Brown—like those long-gone officers who were so jealous of Miles—couldn't wait to get rid of him once the Nez Perce had been beaten. In contrast, Brown devotes page after page to detailed data on dozens of officers who play only minor roles. And in the case of Howard—the commander who failed so many times in the Indian campaigns, whereupon Miles would be sent out to succeed where he had failed—he gives us practically a complete biography: Howard's Civil War exploits, Howard's letters and dispatches, even an

account of all his financial troubles and an analysis of his religious activities.

Yet there is no mention of Miles' even more remarkable
Civil War record, no mention of his private life, and no hint
that he afterward became the top-ranking general of the U.S.
Army. Brown says nothing about Miles' religious convictions,
which, as it happens, were very much in evidence in all his
actions; and this could not be said about poor old Howard,
who tried to make amends for his weaknesses by a zeal for
prayer meetings. Nor is mention made that Miles was enormously popular with the men, privates and officers alike, in his
own command, which had some relevance, one might think,
to his unparalleled record of military victories when the odds
were against him. This is not to say that *The Flight of the Nez
Perce* is badly flawed by the above. It is a very good book, I
think; perhaps the best yet on the subject of this, or any other,
Indian campaign.

The overall tactics of the Nez Perce war involved the migration of the Indians up across Montana in an effort to join the
remnants of the Sioux who had followed Sitting Bull across
the Canadian border, and the frantic efforts of various Army
forces to cut them off and subdue them. Most of the Nez Perce
had come from reservations in Oregon, eluding the troops of
General Howard which had been supposed to contain them.
Howard was ordered to go after them, though this meant he
would be moving into Montana, a part of General Terry's
Department of Dakota. Gibbon, now also a general, and Col.
Sturgis, had already been ordered to join the chase in Terry's
department. Terry was never able to figure out whether or
not these other forces, by being moved into his territory, were
therefore under his command; though afterward he tried to
claim that they had been. To complete the picture of general
confusion, a number of "citizen volunteer" units had been
formed, some numbering a hundred or more men with their
own elected commanders, and these moved about at random,

79

sometimes joining up with one or another of the regular Army units.

The Nez Perce were soon found to be better armed and much more organized than the Sioux had been. In their eastward migration they either badly defeated or stood off every Army unit they encountered. They also killed many settlers and destroyed a number of remote hamlets. The whole Northwest was in a state of panic. This time Sherman decided to step in and issue direct orders himself, bypassing Sheridan. Howard reported that his troops were exhausted and could not push on into the Yellowstone country, and felt it was up to Gibbon, Sturgis (commanding the 7th Cavalry after Custer's death), Miles and others to carry on. Sherman promptly rebuked him and ordered him to continue.

It seems to have been Sherman's hope that the forces under Howard, Gibbon, or Sturgis, any or all of them, could overtake the Nez Perce. He had learned in the Sioux campaign that these larger units were often ineffectual in this type of warfare and that Miles' command alone had saved that operation from failure. Still he believed that this time, under his personal direction, the other commanders could defeat the Nez Perce before they reached Miles' territory north of Fort Keogh. But the Nez Perce easily kept far ahead of Howard's troops. Along the way they were intercepted by General Gibbon's command, and while they were encamped, Gibbon attacked. The resulting Battle of Big Hole was the bloodiest of the campaign.

When the Nez Perce squaws fought as savagely as the warriors, the soldiers began to slaughter them and their children. The enraged braves regrouped outside their camp and counterattacked, driving Gibbon back with severe losses. Out of his whole force of some 140 soldiers and 50 volunteers, 40 were killed and many wounded, some to die later. Only the lucky arrival of reinforcements from another command saved Gibbon's outfit from total annihilation.

This brief mention of the Big Hole battle is intended just to give some idea of what had been going on before Miles finally got into the action. It was, in short, a series of blunders, failures, and defeats. But it should be remembered that in this wildly unbalanced period of U.S. expansion, while the robber barons of industry and railroads were amassing fortunes into the hundreds of millions, the Army was so impoverished that it was common practice for generals, even major generals, to personally lead units of only a few hundred men into the wilderness.

Howard never caught up to the Nez Perces, though it has been claimed by many historians that he purposely held back in order to give Miles time to move up ahead of the hostiles and cut them off. Howard himself later gave this explanation. It seems suspect to me for several reasons; among them, Sherman's order to proceed as rapidly as possible, with the added suggestion that if Howard were too old or fatigued he should let someone else take over his command. Leaving the historians to argue about why Howard was so slow, the pertinent fact is that on September 30 Miles discovered the Nez Perce on Snake Creek, at the foot of the Bear Paw Mountains. It was the last chance to stop the Indians before they would reach the safety of the border, only 42 miles north. Miles knew that if he attacked, no supports could reach him for several days, if at all.

Besides his mounted infantry regiment, Miles had been assigned two battalions of cavalry; but there was a good chance the Indians would outnumber the soldiers. There was also the possibility that the Sioux still at large under Sitting Bull might at any time move down from Canada to aid the Nez Perce. If that should happen, Miles' small command would almost certainly be wiped out before Howard or Sturgis could bring up reinforcements.

THERE could not have been a more likely situation for another Little Big Horn. Probably every man in the outfit knew the outcome depended on the experience and skill of the commander, as well as on his personal courage. Certainly experience was never more in evidence than in the way Miles planned and carried out his initial attack. His scouts, some Indian and some white, were so expert they had located the Nez Perce camp and brought back a detailed description of it, without being themselves detected by the Nez Perce sentries. Situated in complicated and very rough terrain along the winding gullies of Snake Creek, the Indians were encamped in four main divisions some hundred yards apart.

By about 9 A.M. on September 30, Miles had moved his whole command up to within sight of the Indians' position, near enough to launch a charge at the gallop. The cavalry went ahead, led by himself, followed by the mounted infantry (his first chance to prove its effectiveness), with the packtrain, field gun, and some supporting troops holding back to see where they would be most needed. Everything depended on that first attack, the two main objectives being to surround the Indians and to capture their herd of horses grazing just outside the camp. These objectives were accomplished, but with heavy losses on both sides. And it was known that some of the warriors had escaped, during the first hour, before the encircling lines of soldiers had been made secure.

The five-day siege that followed was perhaps the toughest operation of Miles' whole career: cold, snowstorms, no shelter for the wounded, the nearest wood for fuel five miles distant, constant day and night vigil to keep the Indians from breaking through the lines. But finally the Nez Perce chief, Joseph, surrendered; this meant that most of the Nez Perce who had escaped would also give up when they heard the news of Joseph's capitulation.

On the night of October 5, when it was certain Joseph was going to surrender, convinced he could make no better terms than those offered, General Howard arrived. But he had with him only an escort of ten men. There appears to be no official explanation, but from all accounts it would seem that when Howard learned Miles was engaging the Indians, he took his fastest horses and a few men who knew the country best and dashed ahead. And I suppose on finding the victory practically assured, he sent back orders for his command to rest.

Miles stated that he had the worst scare of his life (though those who knew him best held that it was impossible to scare him) when at a critical stage of the battle, while it was snowing hard, a scout reported a long column of Sioux approaching. But as Miles prepared to meet this disastrous development, an officer with field glasses rushed up to say that the scout had seen a herd of buffalo. In his *Recollections* Miles gives a lucidly clear eight-page account of the battle. After checking it against many other accounts and official records, to me it seems highly accurate. Far from playing up his own actions as the commanding officer, his impersonal references to himself are objective and very modest compared to the high praise accorded him by the statements of many who were on the scene.

Yet for some reason Mark Brown, in his book, seems to find ways of denigrating Miles at every turn. A special tone is re-

83

served for Miles which is markedly different from that used in referring to all the other commanders throughout the book, including some who were notoriously incompetent. I must stress this in some detail, because nothing could more directly illustrate my thesis that a curious and long series of events caused a huge myth to be built about the old Indian fighter—a myth which has been believed by scholars and writers up to the present, and which has played a part in obscuring the real Miles from the pages of history. One concrete way of showing this is to quote from what has been written about Miles in certain recent books; and the first I have chosen is Brown's *Flight of the Nez Perce*, because it deals with this important episode in Miles' career.

The Snake Creek battle is the climax of Brown's saga, in a chapter he calls "Six Grim Days." I thought this would mean six grim days for the Nez Perce, since they were defeated; but no, Brown is referring to Miles' troops. It strikes me that, by injecting prejudiced comments, he has also made those six days sound like a grim event in the life of Nelson A. Miles.

Brown starts off: "In the first half hour of action, Miles lost—in killed and wounded—twenty percent of his force. Such a loss might be tolerated if it purchased a victory, but this one had not. Apparently, the enemy was as formidable as ever." If we examine this curious statement in light of the facts, even facts later shown by Brown himself, we can only find that the initial loss of men *was* indeed "tolerated." And it certainly had to be, if Miles were to go on to victory instead of retreating. Furthermore, it was a necessary loss. Neither Brown nor anyone else has ever suggested how else Miles could have surrounded a superior force in a protected and highly defensible position, as well armed as his own men, and known to be the equal of army sharpshooters in marksmanship. The assault had to be made, and quickly, whatever the loss. It was Miles' only chance.

At the same time, the entire operation was dependent upon

84

capturing the Nez Perce horses, so that the Indians couldn't escape easily or engage in the mounted warfare at which they excelled. Only without their horses could they be held at bay. Of course, the initial loss of men had not "purchased a victory" during the first half hour of the fighting; but long before the end of the siege it was more than clear that the first attack, in spite of its losses, *had* been the decisive factor in ultimate victory.

It seems odd that at this point of his story Brown makes no mention of the heavy Nez Perce losses, perhaps even greater than the Army's. After losing many killed and wounded, with their horses all captured, surrounded, and contained on all sides, the Nez Perce were apparently "as formidable as ever." It was certainly not apparent to Miles, fortunately. He knew he had the Nez Perce licked that first day, barring only the arrival of the Sioux before he could conclude his siege and reduce Joseph to the point of surrendering. It was learned afterward that, as Miles suspected, the Nez Perce had sent emissaries to ask the Sioux for help. But on hearing that the Army was so near, the Sioux had decided instead to move farther back into Canada. Probably they knew that Miles, who had always beaten them, was leading the forces they would meet if they went to aid the Nez Perce.

In Brown's detailed and dramatic chapter about the six-day battle on Snake Creek, the nearest thing to a compliment he accords the commander is served up second hand. It occurs in a quote from an account written by the regimental surgeon. "Our gallant commander, on a splendid steed, is here, there, everywhere. When the first horse is blown a fresh one is mounted, and off again. Three horses are ridden down during the day; their rider never appears to tire."

In Miles' own account of the battle, he gives a clear picture of the situation at 5:30 P.M. of the first day: "I felt positive we had secured the beleaguered Indians in their camp beyond the possibility of escape. I did not, therefore, order a general assault, as I knew it must result in the loss of many valuable lives and possibly might end in a massacre. [It should be noted here that Miles was violently opposed to the tactics of officers who massacred Indians in their camps. It was well known that the Nez Perce squaws and quite young children would fight savagely when cornered and could often handle firearms as effectively as the braves. In this case, he probably meant that assaulting the camp would result in the killing of women and children, rather than in the massacre of his own men by the Indians.] The Indians occupied a crescent-shaped ravine, and it was apparent that their position could only be forced by a charge or a siege. The first could not be accomplished without too great a sacrifice, while the latter in my judgement would be almost sure to result satisfactorily. My one concern then was . . . the Sioux. . . ." He goes on to explain in detail the position of the Sioux and how he concluded that the Nez Perce who had escaped would probably try to bring them down to aid their besieged allies. "I, therefore, desired that the military authorities should have some intimation of my position, and to that end sent word to General Terry, commanding the department, who was then in Fort Benton, nearly a hundred miles to the west, apprising him of our movements and success. I also sent orders to Colonel Sturgis to move up and join us without delay. He was then a hundred miles to the south and separated from us by the Missouri River. I likewise informed General Howard of our position."

There was still some sharp skirmishing going on when Miles sent out his couriers, and he was still riding around the lines, improving the positions of his men and taking care of the wounded. It was getting colder and snowing. Doubtless he gave most of his information verbally, but this written message survives; it was intended primarily for Sturgis.

I have this day surprised the hostile Nez Perce in their camp, and have had a sharp fight. I have several officers and men wounded (about 30). About 25 Indians are still in their camp, which is well protected.

We captured most of their herd. But I may have trouble in moving on account of my wounded. Please move forward with caution and rapidity.

Commenting on this hastily scribbled but carefully thought-out message Miles sent Sturgis, Brown remarks: "Perhaps this was as near as the proud colonel could come to saying that he had a bear by the tail, and did not know what to do with it." What could have motivated such a remark? There is nothing in any of the contemporary diaries, journals, or reports, including those quoted by Brown, to give the slightest indication that Miles, even granted he could be said to have had a bear by the tail, "did not know what to do with it."

At one point Brown speculates at some length on whether the Nez Perce ponies captured numbered 700, as some observers reported, or, as others estimated, 800. The number may have been a matter of some interest to the Nez Perce in 1878, as they were to be given back the ponies after surrendering their arms and promising to fight no more. What is of interest to *me* is why, though quoting at length from obscure diaries and journals, Brown ignores Miles' own precisely stated account of the Nez Perce affair. The only hint I find lies in his preoccupation with statistics, again with regard to horses. Brown mentions that years afterward, in writing of the charge which opened the battle, Miles referred to the sound of 600 horses galloping over the prairie. Then Brown adds flatly, ". . . but this is a gross exaggeration." He attempts to prove his point by counting the number of mounted infantry, cavalry units, scouts, and so on; and apparently assuming there could be but one horse to a man, he concludes that the fighting force of 350 could not have had 600 horses.

In thus casting doubt on Miles' veracity, Brown has chosen what I feel is a poor argument. In the 1870's, the Indian-fighting colonel of the 5th Infantry was already well known, and thoroughly disliked by some, for being a stickler when it came to precise figures in military matters. And Brown says nothing about how many horses there may have been in the supply train of forty wagons which followed the charge up to a point near the firing line. Four, or even six, to a wagon, perhaps? What about a reasonable number of spare mounts and pack-horses? So I see no reason to doubt the word of the expert horseman who developed the "mounted infantry," and who all his life was as accustomed to counting horses as any plains-man or rancher.

Perhaps the strangest affront of all is a line in Brown's sum-ming up of the events of the first day of battle: "Although Miles knew that he had part of the Indians cornered, he was fearful and jittery." Well! Even among his worst enemies, from the Apaches to the Spaniards, and among his detractors, from Hearst jingoists to Theodore Roosevelt, I know of none who ever found Miles fearful of anything, let alone jittery. And if he was jittery after winning the first round of the bat-tle, it was not observed by any of his surviving 330 men or by the Nez Perce whom he had surrounded.

It also seems to have been conveniently forgotten that Miles was not acting in any way on his own initiative in this cam-paign, though he may have done so in others. He had been handed direct and specific orders, from Sherman himself, to pursue the Nez Perce as rapidly as possible and to attack them if he could—whether or not there were any other troops near enough to support him, and whether or not the Nez Perce might have a force superior to his own. That Miles sent word to Howard and Sturgis asking for reinforcements seems to me the only sound and sensible course possible under the circum-stances, not evidence that he was "fearful and jittery."

Miles could have pressed on into the hostiles' camp and killed them all, with the probable loss of a few more soldiers. To wait it out, with the Sioux known to be nearer than any supporting troops, was a calculated risk. By taking the latter course Miles prevented the needless slaughter of the encircled Nez Perce and avoided the loss of any more of his own men. For this he was highly commended by his immediate superior, Howard, and also by Sherman.

I do not question the sincerity of any recent writers on the subject. They must have been influenced at some point during their researches, I feel sure, by the many false statements and insinuations of Miles' influential enemies. When a certain sort of adverse publicity becomes a popular myth, it keeps on being repeated long after those who invented it have been forgotten. And along the way, some writers, taking the myth for fact, see no harm in adding a few strengthening touches of their own.

The circumstances of the final surrender of Chief Joseph seem to mark a signal point in the life of Nelson A. Miles. For from this time onward, Miles became a figure who inspired violent disagreement. Out of this disagreement grew a situation which led to myth succeeding myth; and then, when even the myths were almost forgotten, to the strange disappearance of the real identity of the man who had inspired them.

10

THE day after Howard arrived with his small escort on the
bleak scene of the siege at Snake Creek, Chief Joseph
came out under a flag of truce. Howard, though outranking
Miles, allowed the colonel the honor of accepting the Indians'
surrender.

This has been accepted generally as purely an act of courtesy
on Howard's part. (Brown gives him high praise.) But after
studying many contemporary accounts, it occurs to me there
may also have been other reasons. For one thing, Howard
might have looked not a little vain in the eyes of all those
tough and battle-weary men, accepting the surrender when he
had arrived too late to be of any help. Not to mention the adverse publicity he would surely receive when news of the affair reached the outside world. He may also have feared that
if he should step in at that delicate stage of negotiations, Joseph might change his mind. Lastly and most important, General Howard knew from past experience that the government
would probably welsh on the terms Miles had been authorized to offer the Indians—fair treatment as prisoners of war,
etc.—and the general may not have wanted to be caught with
the unpleasant responsibility for trying to see that those terms
would be carried out.

In any case, it is a matter of record that Miles went out of his way to put in writing a formal expression of thanks to Howard for not superseding him on this occasion. But long after the command had returned to civilization, an aide of General Howard, Lieutenant Wood, a rather vain young man who felt that Miles had slighted him in some way when they arrived at Snake Creek, started a strange rumor which was picked up by the newspapers. This story has been repeated, with varying degrees of credence, in just about every account of the Nez Perce campaign ever written (though it has been pointed out by several that Wood was known to be a heavy drinker and a spinner of wild yarns).

According to Wood's tale, he was present at Snake Creek when Miles showed Howard the dispatch he had just written informing his department commander, General Terry, of Joseph's surrender. Wood said that Howard read the message and approved its contents by some smiling remark to Miles. The latter then took the dispatch, Wood continued, and some distance back of the lines handed it to a courier; and in doing this he was gone twenty minutes or so. Wood's conclusion was that Miles probably substituted a different dispatch. The point being that the first had mentioned Howard's presence at Snake Creek, while the second had not.

It is a fact that the brief dispatch to Terry did not state that Howard was present. For this Miles was accused of discourtesy and glory seeking by some, in the subsequent hassle over who should get the credit for the victory. Perhaps this dispute gave Wood the idea for his malicious speculation that Miles had shown Howard one dispatch and then sent out a different one.

Brown, though he had previously found Wood considerably less than reliable, writes: "Wood believed that Miles substituted this message which gave to him all the glory associated with the final surrender." And thus he has added to the perpetuation of the mythical Miles, the glory hunter. There is no evidence whatever that Wood really "believed" his own drunken yarn; and it should be noted that he didn't present his theory as a fact, but merely as guesswork.

The Wood yarn is so full of loopholes they are perhaps mostly apparent. How could Miles' "glory" possibly be enhanced by not mentioning Howard's presence, especially since the latter had not asked for the honor of receiving Joseph's surrender? Why should it be assumed that Miles ought to have informed Terry at headquarters that Howard had finally arrived? Under such circumstances, indeed any circumstances, it is hardly an accepted military procedure for a colonel to report on the presence and activities of a general. Presumably Howard, if he wished his position known at that moment, would send his own dispatches; and if he chose not to, he would in any case report fully in person on his return a few days later. Then, too, if Miles had shown Howard a fake dispatch, Howard was certainly not a man to keep silent about it, nor would he have reason to, once he had discovered such a clumsy trick had been played. And Miles, of course, would have foreseen such inevitable exposure, if he had been capable of the improbable deception. Nor would he have been likely to write his wife, as he did on the same day, casually remarking after telling her of the victory, "General Howard arrived last night," if he had wanted to conceal the fact.

Yet Brown states that Howard, when he saw no reference to himself in Miles' dispatch as it appeared in the newspapers, "was deeply hurt by this selfish glory-grabbing." Howard may have been deeply hurt, but for reasons other than Miles' "glory-grabbing." The unfortunate psalm-singing general, never noted for his tact, was berated by Terry, in a letter to Sheridan, for issuing orders to Miles relative to the handling of Nez Perce prisoners. Miles was supposed to receive orders through Terry—Howard had no authority outside his own command while in Terry's Department of Montana. Then Howard was hauled up by Sheridan and given a violent rebuke for having stated in a newspaper release that Sheridan had expressed the opinion that credit for defeating the Nez Perce should be shared among Howard, Gibbon, Miles, and Sturgis. In fact, Sheridan had already reported officially that Miles had been responsible for the final victory by his brilliant action at Snake Creek.

For several months after Chief Joseph's defeat at Snake Creek, the ruckus continued among the various Army commanders and their respective supporters about who was entitled to the credit. This bickering was greatly stimulated by prominent newspaper correspondents, whose accounts of interviews with the officers involved were often more sensational than truthful. There should have been little question about the matter: Every commander in the area had direct orders from Sherman to intercept the Indians if possible; Miles did so and defeated them, his command unaided during the five-day fight. So the credit belonged to Miles, and indirectly to Sherman as the overall commander.

Some of the other officers, however, decided that Miles was getting altogether too much fame for his exploits at Snake Creek. They gave out statements to the effect that General Howard's men had exhausted the Indians during his long pursuit of them, aided by Sturgis' efforts. Howard himself, who had often been ridiculed in the newspapers for having let the Nez Perce get around him in his own department and for never engaging any numbers of them in battle on his chase eastward, then came out with a masterpiece of second-guessing. He proclaimed that he had slowed down his pursuit of the Nez Perce so that they would travel more slowly, enabling Miles to catch up to them. If this were true, it would seem a strange course to follow just after his receiving an impatient order from Sherman to press on with all possible speed and the curt suggestion that if he were too tired to go on, he should relinquish his command to someone who could keep up the pace.

To prove his theory that it had been his own brilliant maneuvering which had enabled Miles to trap the Indians, Howard cited a dispatch he had sent Miles before the Snake Creek battle. In this message, which was sent only after Howard learned the Indians had got a whole week's march ahead of him, he urged Miles to hurry northward to try to intercept Chief Joseph's forces, adding that he was "holding back" in order not to press the Indians on into Canada before Miles could catch up to them.

Howard, a religious fanatic, was courageous and ambitious but notoriously ignorant of Indian tactics. He was an erratic and vacillating commander and had had a dismal record of failures as an Indian fighter ever since the Civil War. No one knew this better than Miles, who liked Howard personally but had made a study in some detail of all the reasons for his lack of success against the Indians. Miles denied Howard's lame assertion that his delay had been planned so that Miles could overtake the Nez Perce, and hence Howard should share half the credit for the victory!

No one has explained how Howard could possibly have foreseen that Miles would make one of the fastest marches in the military history of the West—by using his just-invented mounted infantry—or how Howard could have known that Miles would be able to locate the exact position of the Nez Perce in a wilderness extending for hundreds of miles in all directions. Howard himself had never known how to make any such effective use of scouts or how to glean intelligence from friendly Indians. Last of all, why should Howard have been so confident that Miles, with only 350 men, would be able to defeat a band of Indians he had often reported as numbering at least a thousand, and possibly two thousand?

For almost two years after the close of the Nez Perce campaign, until 1880, Miles was embroiled in a struggle to relocate and permanently settle the defeated and demoralized tribe. As always, he took the part of the Indians against their dual enemy, the War Department and the politicians. The government sent a large number of Nez Perce down to Oklahoma reservations, against Miles' protests. Soon many were dying from the unfamiliar climate and intolerable living conditions. Miles finally shamed and threatened the authorities into moving the survivors back north.

There was also a great fight about the matter of trying many of the warriors for murder. The Northwestern states all pressed for such an action; the settlers wanted revenge for all of their number who had been killed in the revolt. Miles opposed them in Washington and finally got most of the trials indefinitely postponed. The affairs of the Nez Perce were at last settled, except for minor details, when in 1880 some of the former lands of the Indians were restored to them in Utah and Oregon. In part due to Miles' efforts, the remnants of the displaced tribes were located there.

Brown rushes through all this in the last six or seven pages of his book. No inconsistency with glory grabbing is seen in Miles' two-year struggle to get a fair deal for the Nez Perce. Nothing unusual is noted in the fact that the Indians' cause was being supported by a mere colonel, while generals and major generals in the chain of command above him were doing little or nothing. And no notice is taken that, ironically, the only commander ever to defeat them in war afterward became their champion and most active defender in their last battle—the battle with politicians and racists who wanted them exterminated.

Still, I am very greatly indebted to *The Flight of the Nez Perce*. More than any other, it was this book, with its background of extensive and detailed research, that filled in most of the missing clues as to when and how the myth of Miles the glory hunter began. I am sure now that it all started with the acrimonious intra-army intrigues following Miles' victory over the Nez Perce, and with attempts by certain other officers to capitalize on that victory for their own interests. It is of only secondary concern here that Brown accepts the Miles of the myth that began in 1878 and adds to it, while I have found an entirely different Miles. What matters is how and why one of the major figures in our military history continues to be almost forgotten, while some of his contemporaries of lesser rank and accomplishment are much better known.

11

MY own picture of Nelson Miles toward the end of the 1870's is quite a happy one. In his early forties, his big frame was still lean and hard as ever. He was still romantically in love with Mary, more devoted to her than ever, and she shared all his various interests with real enthusiasm. He had been recommended for promotion, and this time there were hints that Mary's Uncle Cump Sherman might really come through with it. At times angry and frustrated at the repeated tales of his "glory seeking" after Snake Creek, Miles was not deeply upset. He had no doubts he was entirely in the right, and he had plenty of good friends on his side.

His detractors seem not to have considered that Miles was by no means thinking only of himself or of his chances for a promotion. All his life he regarded it as an obligation of military life to take the utmost pride in any command. Therefore Miles would always lash out with any means at hand, and not always very diplomatically, against anyone who sought to deprive his *command*—not just himself—of any credit he thought justly due. In the case of the Snake Creek battle, he was more than ordinarily concerned because of the officers and enlisted men who had been killed, some of them old and dear friends.

The squabble about credit for the Nez Perce defeat was finally ended abruptly by Sherman himself, who lost all pa-

97

tience with Howard and others. He issued a direct order to every commander in the Northwest area to desist, either verbally or in writing, from all further discussion of the matter. But the records were there, in old newspapers, letters, and military reports, for historians to exhume forever afterward.

In December, 1880, Sherman finally put his fears of nepotism aside and rewarded Miles with the long-sought promotion to brigadier general. For the Mileses, the pleasure in this honor was somewhat heightened by realization that, after thirteen years, housekeeping on the woefully inadequate salary of a colonel was ended. Thirteen years, by the way, is quite a long time to spend fighting Indians—or fighting anybody. In all our history, when the shooting starts, four or five years is about par for the course, except for the Indian campaigns. In 1880 Miles still had another ten years or so of Indian fighting ahead of him.

Even though historians long ago lost track of General Miles as one of the more remarkable commanders-in-chief of the U.S. Army since Washington's time—and such statements were often made about him in the early 1900's—he certainly should have received lasting prominence for being the most durable. Custer was a folk hero, so the Little Big Horn story gets told and retold; but over the years, before and after that event, hundreds of other officers and thousands of their men managed to end their careers in much the same manner as Custer. The Indians were especially fond of trying out their aim on officers; and by surviving their fire for some twenty years, Miles, according to the firm belief of the Sioux, possessed a magic power that made him bulletproof.

Apparently Miles is better remembered by descendants of the tribes he had to fight than by his own race. I recently received a note from a Western friend who had been in Nez Perce country, to the effect that some of the kids of that tribe can be heard to chant, even today, something like "Miles you!" as the greatest taunt they could possibly use.

It is time, I think, to take a breather in the strictly narrative approach to the affairs of General Miles. What has been written so far is an extremely condensed impression gleaned from a considerable amount of reading, plus whatever I had picked up at random over the years, since first noticing that eagle-eyed old gentleman peering down at me from the wall of the Westminster library and wondering who he was. A few thousand items which seemed irrelevant, or dull, or just too long-winded, have been shoved aside. But in such wholesale discarding, some bits and pieces have been skipped over which perhaps should have been mentioned. On going through several beer cartons of old notes, I find the following:

Several references to Old Jack, Miles' setter. Jack, who must have been a fine bird dog, once found water when Miles' men were almost dying of thirst on a desert march in the Kiowa-Comanche campaign. He became lost during a battle with the Indians and made his way, about a hundred miles through the wilderness, back to Miles' base camp. Miles often wrote Mary about Old Jack's exploits.

Note: Trees. A born woodsman and something of a botanist, Miles used his knowledge to train his men in the art of surviving in winter campaigning—how to find and prepare proper wood for fires means the difference between life and death when encamped in temperatures 40 to 50 below zero. One who knew at a glance the nature of forest growth could use that forest to greatest advantage in establishing defensive positions, etc. Most West Point-trained commanders were at a great disadvantage compared to Indians in this respect.

Note: Love life. Miles has never appealed to any of the romantic historical novelists as a subject. Maybe because he was a one-woman man, having no premarital nor extramarital relations with the ladies to be parlayed into best-seller material.

99

How can you concoct an exciting romance about such a happily married man and his devoted wife, even when that wife is as beautiful and accomplished as Mary? If they ever had an argument, they kept it to themselves.

Note: Just heard one of Professor Eric Goldman's television talk-shows—guests, head of Indian affairs in Washington (himself an Indian) and a Sioux chief. Goldman asks: What exactly *should* the government decide to do in a current controversy in Congress relating to use of a Sioux reservation in the Northwest? Sioux chief's rather heated reply: What business is it of the U.S. government to be doing *anything at all* with lands belonging entirely and legally to the Indians? (Point: Indians being treated no more fairly today than a century ago; just being cheated in a more sophisticated manner.) On this same issue of the Sioux land, Miles jeopardized his career in the 1870's by going to Washington of his own volition and taking the part of the Sioux—any career Army officer of today like to try this?

Note: 1870-1890, only ten or so active brigadier generals in whole U.S. Army. Paid bare subsistence wages. Army so cut down in numbers, generals Howard and Terry, in Sioux campaign, each had only about a thousand men in their commands. Yet Army was supposed to make whole West safe for white man's development, with uncounted thousands of hostile or potentially hostile Indians roaming almost at will. Meanwhile "robber barons" of industry, railroads, and mining making hundreds of millions of dollars.

Even general officers without private funds have a hard time; Howard twice investigated for doubtful financial deals, trying to become solvent again after going broke. Miles must have been aided by some money from Mary's side of the family, but he was too independent to accept more than a minimum necessary to support his wife and two children. (Son, Sherman, born 1882.) Tried to make some money in mining stocks, but lost.

Note: Miles arrives at Custer's headquarters soon after the massacre and finds 27 new widows there. Points out his and Mary's great concern for Elizabeth Custer, who was one of them. Etc.

Note: The Indians call Miles "Bear Coat" after he proves winter campaigning can be carried out in Montana.

Note: Mention excellent book, *A Gallery of Dudes,* by Marshall Sprague—especially chapter about Prince Maximilian's ethnic studies in the Old West. Finds fur traders and scouts prefer Cree squaws, not because of their beauty or cooking but because they generate more heat in bed, thus insuring against freezing to death on subzero trips in Montana country. . . . No evidence Miles ever resorted to this himself, however; too much of a New England puritan, I guess.

Note: Yellowstone Park. When Miles went in 1878 to survey scene of Custer's Last Stand, he took along his family and some other guests for a scenic camping trip. Most people today think National Parks were inaugurated by Theodore Roosevelt, and maybe Pinchot, in early 1900's. (T.R. himself certainly helped this impression.) The Yellowstone had been made a National Park in 1872. Quite a number of the first hardy tourists to make sightseeing excursions there were killed by Indians. It was in September, 1888, that Miles surprised a hostile band of Bannocks in the Park and defeated them, losing two of his own men and killing eleven Indians.

Note: Miles had the annoying habit, throughout his whole military career, of never losing a fight. It made things difficult for all those who disliked him or were jealous of him. It also made historians anxious to forget him. How do you explain a man like that? Maybe the only military man we like less than one we decide was to blame for losing some important battle is one who has never lost any battles at all.

As shown in many letters to Mary during the years before 1880, at the end of each successive Indian campaign Miles thought that perhaps *this* time he would be rewarded with a promotion. But Sherman stubbornly continued to refuse all pressures on this point. (I cannot prove it, but I am quite sure in my own mind that Sherman really hoped Miles would get discouraged and quit the Army entirely.) Once, when Miles had carried out several successful operations against the Indians, after the general officers above him had tried and failed, he approached Sherman directly about a promotion. Sherman offered him a desk job in Washington, saying that if Miles would accept this, a promotion might be arranged.

Sherman was obviously annoyed when Miles refused to take his advice. But Miles knew that a desk job, in those days, was a good way for an officer to disappear from the public eye forever. If it ever should lead to a promotion, it would only be to brigadier in something like the Quartermaster Corps, after some older incumbent was retired for age, and he would end his career as an obscure lowest-rank general.

Miles had long since set his sights on the top position, and in this he was constantly encouraged by his wife. He believed that if he could pile up a succession of well-publicized victories in the field, the day would come when Sherman could no longer find any excuse for not promoting him on his record alone. One defeat, however, one ambush in which his command would get the worst of it from the Indians, and his chances would doubtless be finished—if he didn't stop an Indian bullet himself along the way.

All the evidence suggests that for years Sherman regarded his nephew-in-law as a problem, and at times an acute embarrassment. Miles' occasional personal letters to him about the operational shortcomings of various general officers in the Western commands must have sorely vexed the commander-in-chief. The West Point-trained officers did not do this sort of thing. But at the same time, the West Pointers didn't have much luck when the Indian fighting got serious. Custer had been the Army's white hope; but when he was wiped out, it was suddenly plain the whole concept of Indian fighting must be drastically overhauled.

After the massacre, the consensus among the field commanders in the West was that they needed much larger forces, but, as Sherman uncomfortably knew, the Army had neither the manpower nor the funds to put larger forces in the field. And the problems of supply and communications, and above all the lack of experience in wilderness fighting techniques, made the use of large forces almost impossible even if they could be obtained. Also, after the massacre, Sherman started to explain that he hadn't promoted Miles because he feared Miles was too "rash" in leading his small command against the Indians, especially when he knew he was outnumbered. It was generally thought, at least privately, in the higher echelons of the Army, that Custer had met his end because he had been too rash—overconfident, in other words.

So Sherman waited another two years, while Miles went on fighting, and winning, against the Sioux, the Nez Perce, and the Bannocks. Finally, in 1880, when it had become obvious to everybody in the United States who could read newspapers that Miles was the ablest Indian fighter the Army had ever seen, Sherman put him up for promotion to brigadier general. The promotion arrived in December, and Brig. Gen. Nelson A.

103

Miles was assigned to command the Department of the Columbia. It was a country that fascinated him, and he was delighted at the prospect; there he would be able to ride herd on the officials responsible for the welfare of the Nez Perce who had been returned to their Western reservations.

12

IF I had not happened to write the Westminster town history, and had become aware of General Miles through some other circumstance, my impression of the man at this stage of his career almost certainly would have been quite different. But in any town history it is more or less implicit that personalities are described, if not flatteringly, at least in the most favorable light possible without distorting the facts. In a town being thus memorialized, almost everybody who ever lived there is wholly admirable. The only bad people died long ago and have no descendants still in town.

So in writing a chapter about Westminster's most illustrious native son, it was my job to dig up all his accomplishments and to portray his virtues. And if some musty old papers had turned up showing that Miles was less than virtuous, it would not have been mentioned in my history. As a matter of fact, many of the references found in the beginning of my search were distinctly unflattering. So too were the impressions of older people who remembered something about Miles—usually something they had read about him in the newspapers during the aftermath of the Spanish-American War. (Nobody seemed to know what he had done after that, and most were surprised to learn that he had lived until 1925.) In one scholarly and celebrated work, published in 1959, I found a long diatribe which included the line: "A born troublemaker and tireless promoter of his own interests. . . ."

This was not the sort of thing to bring any great joy to my good friends of the Westminster Historical Society. And I remember thinking that this same writer surely would never have gone so far out of the way to make such nasty remarks about any other commanders of the U.S. Army, whatever their shortcomings. So what monstrous wrongdoing had Miles been guilty of, to inspire such treatment?

I could find nothing at all of any consequence; and the more I read, the less I found. But there wasn't time enough to go into the matter very deeply. I read Miles' books; and I read much of what had been written about him, but that didn't seem to be too much. Nobody had as yet written a biography of him. I had ample evidence that the unfavorable comments could not have resulted logically from his lack of ability or success as a military commander. Miles was nothing if not eminently successful in all his military engagements, and in several important peacetime assignments as well. There was never the slightest hint of irregularities in his personal life or his private affairs. And that was about as far as I could go then.

After the history was finished, I occasionally ran across some further reference to Miles; and friends in college American history departments sent me items from time to time. One day it occurred to me there was something quite strange in the chronological sequence of all those references. Starting back around 1900, for a few years many of the references, indeed all the impersonal and more or less historical ones, such as found in almanacs, encyclopedias, and histories, were glowing tributes. (For example, a 1906 atlas, with a special section of biographical sketches, portrays Miles as one of the greatest Army commanders in U.S. history, whose crowning achievement had been, against great odds, managing to prevent the Spanish-American War from turning into a national disaster.)

Some of this sort of thing continued to be printed, or re-printed, as long as the old gentleman was still living. But from 1925 to the present, all the references become increasingly critical. In recent years, whenever someone has had occasion to mention Miles, the fact that he once was top commander of the Army, let alone during a war, has begun to be left out entirely. So it might be concluded that whatever the reasons for Miles' unpopularity in some quarters during his own time, the same reasons probably apply even more today. And the same sort of people who disliked him then would dislike him more today. History has always been a telescope, but we are never quite sure which end we are looking through.

At the peak of his career, Miles, like General Douglas Mac-Arthur in a later time, was a popular hero and greatly admired by a large segment of the public, though despised by others, including certain powerful interests in and out of the government. But after his death the impression created by his enemies lived on, while the impression of his friends has faded almost to the vanishing point. How much of this we can explain will be seen after we have followed the General through the period of the Spanish-American War.

While working on the Westminster story, I had written Maj. Gen. Sherman Miles, then retired, asking for whatever data he might wish to contribute. (I did not meet him personally until some years later.) In replying, he mentioned that his father's letters were on loan to Mrs. Virginia W. Johnson, who was writing a full-length biography of Nelson A. Miles. The book, called *The Unregimented General*, was published in 1962. I did not get around to reading it until two or three years later, not having considered writing anything further about Miles at the time.

The biography turned out to be quite a surprise. I suppose I had expected it would explain all the mystery enshrouding the banishment of Miles from his once prominent place in the pages of our history. But it seems that no matter how impressive the amount of research, as evidenced by a lengthy bibliography, one just doesn't find the key to the Miles puzzle in old War Department records. This book told me nothing of consequence I did not already know about the General.

The author, a native of Montana and a devotee of frontier history, was interested in Miles mainly as the paramount Indian fighter of that region. Her book disposes of Miles' background and his life up to age twenty in exactly two pages. (Out there, history begins around 1870.) The next thirty pages cover the Civil War and events leading to Miles' first Indian campaign. Then come two hundred and sixty-six pages of Indian fighting; and only thirty pages taking Miles from 1890 through the Spanish-American War and to his death in 1925.

The title itself suggested to me that Mrs. Johnson must have somehow acquired an impression of Miles very different from my own. Even from my first acquaintance with him in the records of Westminster, I had found him to be the most completely regimented character I had ever run across: in his boyhood and somewhat puritanical background; in his philosophy and dedication to military education; in his formal and perhaps even rather pompous approach to all military protocol and procedures; in all his writings, even his love letters to Mary; in his rigid code of ethics and Federalist political convictions; in his lifelong almost total reserve and reticence in all personal matters. In every aspect of his life, it seems to me, the Miles approach was synonymous with regimentation.

By far the greater part of Mrs. Johnson's story follows Miles as a colonel and brigadier general during his Indian fighting days, and the author's enthusiasm for her subject is almost unbounded. But this enthusiasm falters immediately after Miles has been made commander-in-chief of the Army. Then the author apologetically begins looking for character flaws to explain every setback or controversy her hero runs into, every political fight in which he is involved. We are reminded that

Miles was utterly lacking in "tact," and that he was incurably "undiplomatic."

Surely there is something ambivalent here. In Mrs. Johnson's own excellent account of all the Indian campaigns, it is proved beyond question that Miles, alone among all his colleagues, possessed the tact and diplomatic skill to be able to parley successfully with one after another of all the most truculent and difficult of the Indian chiefs. Apparently Mrs. Johnson, believing that tact and diplomacy are the cardinal virtues of the military life, does not consider that Miles, in some of his dealings with stubborn superiors and politicians, may have decided to deliberately throw tact and diplomacy to the four winds. After all, he had to face many situations in which all the tact and diplomacy in the world would have got him nowhere, except perhaps eventual retirement as an obscure brigadier general.

Mrs. Johnson's repeated inference is that Miles' lack of tact kept holding him back, somehow preventing him from attaining greater eminence. She does not suggest how, had Miles employed tact and diplomacy, he could have risen to a higher position than he attained anyway without being endowed with those qualities. The job of commanding general of the Army was top rung on the military ladder in those days; there was no General Staff then.

In the last part of her book, Mrs. Johnson deplores those episodes in which Miles tangles with Washington officials. But the author of *The Unregimented General* is by no means alone in her view that mixing into politics could only leave an indelible blot on the career of a high-ranking general. All Miles' critics, over the years, have taken the same line. Most of them were no less than outraged at the very thought that Miles at one time actually considered running for President. For my part, it would seem to be the last and most significant of all possible tributes to a brilliant life of public service even to have been *suggested* for the Presidency. The fact that

Miles may have thought about having a try at it, if sufficient backing were found, only adds to my admiration for both his courage and his belief in himself.

Whether he would have made a good President or the worst is hardly the point here, but it does suggest an interesting chain of thought. What might have happened if Miles could have found enough backing, and could have been elected? My first surmise is that, at worst, he could hardly have been more inept than some of the Presidents he had served under.

What intrigues me is the effect that Miles, as President, would have had on the treatment of the American Indians. Whatever havoc he might have wrought in any or all other fields, the rights and the future of the Indians would have been his major concern. He would certainly have stirred up such a national storm over the issue that the Indians could not have continued to be quite so abused and ignored as they were under other Presidents for so long.

Whatever Miles might have succeeded in doing for the rights of Indians would have had an impact on the other minorities, most notably the Negroes. (Miles had already championed the cause of equal rights for Negroes in his book of 1896.) The civil rights movement might at least have had some sort of beginning, some recognition at the top level of government, in the early 1900's instead of fifty years later. So therein, for what it's worth, lies another clue to why so many people couldn't wait to shove Miles into the back pages of history. Outspoken defenders of racial minorities were not so popular over half a century ago.

In the winter of 1965 my wife and I were happily exploring, in the old Land Rover, some remote corners of the Everglades. I was writing a lazy series of essays for the Berkshire *Eagle*, a Massachusetts paper which has long employed me whenever

I was in danger of starving. While down there we were invited by an old quail-shooting friend to spend a weekend in Boca Grande. A small village on an island and one of Florida's oldest and most exclusive resorts, Boca Grande was first established as a nitrate port. The business is still carried on at one end of the island, where ships can load. Cleveland Amory once described the resort to a social-climbing hostess as the loveliest fertilizer factory in Florida, or something to that effect.

Is it possible to identify a man in his eighties whom you have never seen before, at first glance, just from having once carefully studied several portraits of his father? Perhaps someone had told me earlier that Sherman Miles was at Boca Grande, but I had no memory of it when we were taken to a cocktail party that afternoon, an intimate little affair of a hundred and fifty or so guests. Anyway, I remember thinking that this man, except for the absence of the sweeping moustache, could have posed for one of the later pictures of Nelson A. Miles. And when I spoke to him, the unusually powerful bass voice, as he replied, cut through that cocktail party din like an amplifier with the volume turned up. It was easy to imagine this was the same voice that had boomed across every parade ground in the West during the Indian campaigns.

The erect military bearing, the commanding tone, the keen appraising eye, would still make him stand out in any company. But the big frame of Maj. Gen. Sherman Miles, Ret., at eighty-three had begun to weaken a good deal, and it was evident he sensed then that he had only about a year or so left. He apologized for sitting down as he asked me to join him over in a corner where we could talk without interruption.

Sherman Miles had been pleased with the profile of his father in the Westminster history. It had been the first time in many years that he had seen anything written about Miles,

Sr., that was not merely repetition of the old myths originated by the anti-Miles journalists and politicians of his youth. He especially liked my comparison of his father to Billy Mitchell, that greatly wronged champion of the Air Force, who only after his death in obscurity was finally reinstated as a national hero.

The famous father had been no asset to the military career of Sherman Miles. First of all, at West Point he could not avoid the relentless and constant pressures that must befall any cadet whose father was the commanding general of the Army. Later on, at the outset of World War I, he had to serve under many staff officers who had known his father all too well. Some of them had admired Nelson A. Miles and some had not.

His biggest trial was his marked resemblance to his father, both in looks and personality. Even at the time of the First World War, his father had begun to be remembered more for his embroilments in political controversy than for his great military accomplishments. Like father, like son—the high command treated Sherman Miles much the same way his father had been treated as a colonel, all those years when William Tecumseh Sherman commanded the Army. However, by the time World War II came along, many of the younger general officers who served with Sherman Miles not only did not know of his relationship to Nelson A. Miles but had no idea of the latter's status in military history, incredible though it may seem.

Proof of this, by the way, came up the other day in a conversation with one of the more important military figures of recent times. In some casual reminiscing, he happened to mention that he had been closely associated with Sherman Miles early in World War II, when the latter general had been head of Army Intelligence in Washington. On learning of my interest in this, he asked me what had been the special distinction of Miles' father. I replied that, among other things, he had been commanding general of the U.S. Army all during the Spanish-American War.

"Oh, I'm sure you're mistaken about that," the general replied. "He probably commanded some expeditionary forces in Cuba. If he had ever been commanding general of the whole Army, especially in wartime, he would be much better known—there haven't been too many of them, you know." I did not press the point.

In my talk with Sherman Miles, I remarked that I had heard he was practically unapproachable by journalists and writers generally. He laughed and said, "Well, you know how they treated the Old Gentleman. Maybe I've been a little biased on that subject!" But he went on to say that he would be glad to tell me anything he knew about his father, now that he was assured my point of view about Nelson A. Miles was generally the same as his own. And he did tell me quite a good deal on that visit to Boca Grande. Unfortunately that was before I had any idea of writing this book, and I did not take any notes. The following year, before I could get in touch with him again, the notice of his death appeared in the Boston papers.

With Sherman Miles gone before the book was under way, my next move was to look up whatever had happened to the other Miles descendants. I knew only that around the time Sherman was in West Point his sister, Cecelia, married Samuel Reber, and that Reber had been a lieutenant colonel in the Spanish-American War. I also had an impression that the son-in-law, like son Sherman, had ended his career as a major general.

The biography of Miles made only the barest mention of Cecelia and Sherman. There was nothing at all about what had happened to the family after Miles' death. There may be no law against this; but for my part there is nothing of much greater interest about any man than to learn something about his descendants, if he had any. For the present, it's about time we get back to 1880 and on with the adventures of the General.

13

UNTIL early in the twentieth century, when the vast con-
struction problems of the Panama Canal made a new
approach necessary, the U.S. Army had always been a police
force and nothing more. Nearly all its own commanders, and
Congress as well, saw the Army only in this light. Therefore,
except in times of major wars, the strength of the Army, and
the amounts of military appropriations, were always reduced
to an absolute minimum.

The Army Engineers Corps was supposed to know how to
build temporary log bridges or rafts, repair wagon wheels, and
dig holes and trenches. In peacetime there was hardly a great
amount of this sort of work to be done, and the engineers
were as inactive as any branch of the military. The huge con-
struction crews of the transcontinental railroad building
period of 1879-1890 were civilian directed and civilian manned.
The Army was only out there to make the rail routes safe from
hostile Indians.

From the beginning of his Western experiences, Miles had
thought the Army should play a much bigger part in the development of the country. But for some twenty years his vig-
orous lobbying in this direction met with no success. Sherman,
and later Sheridan, were firm believers in the old police force
theory. The Army should never, never mix into any civilian
business of any kind. There is no doubt whatever that they

regarded Miles as a radical visionary and a dangerous threat to their whole concept of how the Army should be run. By 1880 they had been forced to admit that he had unique abilities as a field commander against the Indians; but they had no use for his ideas of educating the Indians and involving the Army in the administration of Indian affairs; and they did not share his visions of the Army as an instrument for developing irrigation, mining, and other projects distinctly nonmilitary.

In believing that the Army could be more usefully employed than lying fallow in permanent cantonments, with just an occasional parade drill for exercise, Miles himself never considered his ideas either new or original. He had studied all military history back to its beginnings, and he was familiar with the engineering feats of Caesar's armies during the expansion of the Roman Empire. Few of his contemporaries, in the Army or in Congress, were so well read or farsighted in this respect. Some tried to discredit him as an impractical and arrogant meddler in affairs they considered no business of the Army. This opinion of Miles, we know, has been handed down by their successors even to the present. In the field of administering Indian reservations, however, Miles had begun to make some impression on the federal government. This was one reason he was assigned to command the Department of the Columbia in 1881.

In 1879 he had written an article for the magazine *North American Review*. The piece aroused nationwide interest and may have confounded the journalists who had represented Miles as a glory hunter, a man whose main interest in fighting Indians was to win promotion for himself. I won't quote the entire article here; it is long and detailed, and contains a rundown on Indian history from the landing of Columbus. As a writer, Miles never used one word if he could manage to use ten. But in this he was, of course, only reflecting the popular taste of the times, the wordiest period in all literary history. The following excerpts from the article, called "The Indian

116

Problem," do show, I think, an extraordinary ability to express himself in writing, for a man so largely self-educated and whose life up to age forty had hardly been conducive to literary pursuits.

Strange as it may appear, it is nevertheless a fact that, after nearly four hundred years of conflict between the European and American races for supremacy on this continent, . . . we still have the question presented, "What shall be done with the Indian?" Wise men differ in opinion, journalists speculate, divines preach, and statesmen pronounce it still a vexed question. . . .

The real issue in the question now before the American people is, whether we shall begin again the vacillating and expensive policy that has marred our fair name as a nation and a Christian people, or devise some way of still improving the practical and judicious system by which we can govern a quarter of a million of our population, secure and maintain their loyalty, raise them from the darkness of barbarism to the light of civilization, and put an end forever to these interminable and expensive Indian wars.

In considering the subject it might be well to first examine the causes which governed so long the condition of affairs, and if in doing so the writer shall allude to some of the sins of his own race, it will only be in order that an unbiased judgement may be formed of both sides of the question.

Sitting Bull, the great war chief . . . , said, "there was not one white man who loved an Indian, and not an Indian but who hated a white man."

. . . The more we study the Indian's character, the more we appreciate the marked distinction between the civilized being and the real savage. Yet we shall find the latter is, after all, governed by the impulses and motives that govern all other men. The want of confidence and the bitter hatred always existing between the two races have been engendered by the warfare that has lasted for centuries, and by the stories of bad faith, cruelty and wrong handed down by tradition from father to son until they have become second nature in both.

. . . By war the natives have been steadily driven toward the setting sun—a subjugated, doomed race. In council the Indians have produced men of character and intellect, and orators and diplomats of decided ability, while in war they have displayed courage and sagacity of a high order. Education, science, and the resources of the world have enabled us to overcome the savages, and they are now at the mercy of their conquerors. In our treaty relations most extravagant and yet sacred promises have been given by the highest authorities, and these have been frequently disregarded.

. . . it may be asked if the Indians as a body have made any progress toward civilization, and in the light of past history we would be prompted to reply: Why should they have abandoned the modes of life which Nature had given them, to adopt the customs of their enemies?

. . . in early days the Indian tribes were to a considerable extent tillers of the soil, but by constant warfare, in which their fields were devastated and their crops destroyed, they have become the mere remnant of their former strength . . . pushed west where they subsisted on wild fruits or the flesh of animals.

Looking at the purpose of our government toward the Indians, we find that after subjugating them it has been our policy to collect the different tribes on reservations and support them at the expense of our people. The Indians have in the main abandoned the hope of driving back the invaders of their territory, yet there are still some who cherish the thought, and . . . the most noted leader among them advanced such a proposition to the writer within the last few years. They long stood, and mostly still stand, in the position of unruly children to indulgent parents for whom they have very little respect, at times wrongfully indulged and again unmercifully punished.

. . . Living under the government, yet without any legitimate government [of their own] what better subjects or more propitious fields could be found for vice and crime?

We have committed our Indian matters to the custody of an Indian bureau which for many years was part of the military establishment; but for political reasons and to promote party interests, this bureau was transferred to the department of the interior.

118

. . . Why has our management of Indian affairs been less successful than that of our neighbors across the northern boundary? . . . Their system is permanent, decided and just. The tide
of immigration in Canada has not been as great as along our
frontier. They have been able to allow the Indians to live as
Indians, which we have not, and do not attempt to force upon
them the customs which to them are distasteful.

. . . No body of people whose language, religion, and customs
are so entirely different from ours can be expected to cheerfully
and suddenly adopt our own. The change must be gradual,
continuous, and in accordance with Nature's laws.

. . . we are bound to give the Indians the same rights that all
other men enjoy, and if we deprive them of their ancient priv-
ileges we must then give them the best government possible.
Without any legitimate government, and in a section of country
where the lawless are under very little restraint, it is useless to
suppose that thousands of wild savages thoroughly armed and
mounted can be controlled by moral suasion. Even if they were
in the midst of comfortable and agreeable surroundings, yet
when dissatisfaction is increased by partial imprisonment and
the pangs of hunger—a feeling not realized by one man in a
thousand in our civilized life—it requires more patience and
forbearance than savage natures are likely to possess to prevent
serious outbreaks.

. . . Whenever an emergency arises which has not been foreseen and provided for by Congress, such as failure or destruction of their crops, the President should have power, on the
recommendation of the officer in charge or the governors of the
Territories in which the Indians are living, to order the necessary supplies, as has been done in several instances for the white
people. . . .

A race of savages cannot by any human ingenuity be civilized
and Christianized within a few years of time, neither will 250,000
people with their descendants be entirely exterminated. . . .
The white man and the Indian should be taught to live side by
side, each respecting the rights of the other, and both living
under wholesome laws, enforced by ample authority and with
exact justice. Such a government would be most gratifying and
beneficial to the Indians, while those men who have invested

119

their capital, and with wonderful enterprise are developing . . . the far West, as well as those soldiers who are annually called upon to endure greater exposure and suffering than the troops of any other nation on the globe, would hail with great satisfaction any system that would secure a substantial and lasting peace.

A French anthropologist, Claude Lévi-Strauss, has recently been hailed as the newest prophet among the savants of the world who are trying to trace the evolution of the human intellect. One of his most controversial theories, supported in several of his fascinating books, is the notion that the most primitive peoples are not that way because their minds are simple or "backward." On the contrary, the mental equipment of primitive man, past or present, has generally been equal to that of the most civilized man; and the primitive way of life often requires an assortment of mental skills of the highest order. Also primitive peoples, according to Lévi-Strauss, are governed by moral and ethical codes as highly developed as those of the most civilized societies.

In other words, to maintain a primitive society successfully at a static level for, say, a few thousand years, it may take an order of intelligence as great, or greater, than the different type of intelligence dedicated to the constant shifting and changing of customs we call "progress." This theory may be making a stir in academic circles of Europe and the United States, but one can hardly expect it will have the slightest effect on the traditional arbitrary attitudes of the peoples of the world toward each other.

The fact that Miles, almost a century ago, was trying to promote precisely the same ideas with regard to the still primitive Indian tribes indicates he was one of the most original thinkers of his time. Of course practically nobody of any importance in the 1880's was going to believe Miles' perfectly sincere assurances that many of the savage chiefs he had known were men of great character, intelligence, and even nobility. Such people as were willing to espouse the cause of fair treatment for the Indians were invariably convinced that any solution must include forcing Christianity and "education" on the poor primitive red man by any means possible.

Nor was Miles supported very effectively by the great numbers of sentimentalists of those days, whose knowledge of Indians had come straight from the pages of James Fenimore Cooper and Longfellow and the calendar artists who imitated the paintings of Frederick Remington and George de Forest Brush. Their idea that the noble savage, if only let alone by the white man, would at once revert to an idyllic life in the wilds was unrealistic to say the least. After a couple of hundred years of being plentifully supplied with such benefits of the white man as venereal disease, rotgut liquor, contraband rifles, and easy money for those who would turn against their own kind, plus a certain amount of enforced attendance at mission schools, most Indians had long lost their ancient skills for total self-sufficiency.

So I concede, at this point, that Miles was not a success as a propagandist and reformer in the field of ethnic relations. But I give him a big A for effort, something not done, so far, by our historians. He had arrived on the scene much too late to save the Indians, and too early for his theories about equal rights for Indians to be taken seriously. Essentially a practical man and a man of action, he could always improve any situation where he could direct things in person—sometimes, it seemed, he could almost accomplish miracles—but outside the sphere of his own command, his enemies usually succeeded in discrediting his theories in one way or another.

Miles remained in command of the vast Northwest region, designated by the Army as the Department of the Columbia, until 1885. It was the most important five years in the whole development of Oregon and Washington, a period in which the Great Northern Railroad and the Canadian Pacific lines were built. Hundreds of towns were being founded, while mining, timber, and other industries were growing rapidly.

With his usual energy and independence in the absence of specific orders from the high command, Miles lost no time in reorganizing the whole military establishment of the Northwest along lines very different from those followed before he took over. Old posts were abandoned, and new and better ones were built in more strategic locations. A system of Army canteens was set up; if not the first in the United States, they were a novelty in the Western garrisons. And whenever not otherwise occupied, the troops, led by the engineers corps, laid out and sometimes actually constructed roads into areas where there had been none before.

Miles also sent out many scouting parties to make geographical surveys of the areas in Washington Territory (not yet a state) which were still large blank spaces on the existing maps. The Army also completed a network of telegraph lines connecting the main points of the region, from the Canadian border down into Oregon. There were no serious Indian outbreaks during those five years. But few months passed without the threat of one.

It was the same old story. The fifteen or so reservations in the Department of the Columbia were originally huge tracts, more than ample to support the Indians, many of whom were trying to farm as they were constantly encouraged to do by the Indian affairs people. But each year more and more white settlers moved into the Indian country and took up residence, often laying out whole townships overnight. Then the boundaries of the Indians' land would be shifted, sometimes with the connivance of certain Indians themselves who had been corrupted and would sell out for a few dollars. Pushed off all the best farmlands, the Indians could not raise enough food for themselves and were becoming more and more dependent on government aid. When the allotments were insufficient —and they usually were—the Indians would be tempted to go out on raiding parties.

Miles made a number of trips to Washington, sometimes

taking along with him some of the more influential tribal leaders, in attempts to adjudicate such matters as treaties broken by the government and reservation lands usurped by settlers or miners. There seems no point here in going into any great detail about all this. Nor, for that matter, was there anything else pertaining to Miles' career during the years he commanded the Department of the Columbia that is of much interest to us today.

In 1882 the second and last child was born, named Sherman for Mary's family. Cecelia was then thirteen. Miles was enormously delighted at having a son and at once visualized the new arrival as a cadet at West Point, getting the education he had been denied himself and going on to become a top-ranking general. A dream he would see come true in large part, though Sherman was fated never to duplicate his father's fame and ultimate rank.

14

IN 1886 Miles was transferred back to Leavenworth and put in command of the Department of the Missouri. His last activity before leaving the Northwest was to initiate military surveys of Alaska, which he saw as the country's next, and perhaps eventually most important, frontier. The five years of running the Department of the Columbia had been so successful, and so much had been accomplished, Miles hoped his transfer would mean he was in line for an upcoming vacancy on the major general level. Sheridan and others had recommended him. But Grover Cleveland had become President, and that astute politician was not at all interested in Indians, nor in the one and only Army officer who had always dealt successfully with them in both war and peace.

Cleveland liked yes-men, known quantities, conservative people who could be relied on not to stir up controversies in Washington. So, in spite of entreaties from Miles supporters all over the West, where he was immensely popular and well known by this time, the President finally passed him by and elevated both Terry and Howard to the rank of major general. These older gentlemen had learned, after all the wrangling at the end of the Sioux war in which Miles had come out on top, to keep their mouths firmly shut in Washington.

There wasn't much to do in the Department of the Missouri at this time, and Miles was hardly settled in Leavenworth before Sheridan tagged him for duty in the Southwest. A whole new series of Indian outbreaks was developing from western Texas through New Mexico and Arizona. Crook had been in command of that area ever since the Sioux campaign, in which he had so disgusted Miles with his futile bunglings. Apparently his efforts in the Southwest were no more successful. The Apaches had been thoroughly antagonized, and the Army was having no luck at all in trying to round them up.

The Apaches operated very differently from the more northerly tribes. They could scatter and disappear into blistering desert country in which white men could survive only a few days at best, and reappear weeks later, without warning, at some point hundreds of miles from where they had last been seen. The Apaches had often been chased about by the Army. They were generally pushed westward but never decisively defeated. Nor, so far as was known, had they ever been defeated by any of the other Indian tribes, all of whom were traditionally deathly afraid of them.

Crook called them "human tigers" and claimed they were totally ruthless killers, never taking any prisoners or leaving any wounded alive. They preferred indulging in various forms of slow torture, whenever they could, to outright shooting of their enemies. It had long been accepted by the Army that if you were ever in a spot where capture by these Indians was certain, you should be prepared to shoot yourself at the last moment, and there were many cases of this happening.

Most of the troops who had served a length of time in Apache country had seen the tangible evidence of what befell soldiers or civilians when taken alive by the Apaches. Bodies found hanging by the thumbs from a tree or ledge revealed that the arms had been neatly broken before the victims had been strung up. The Apaches had many other little games they liked to play with live prisoners, such as partly disemboweling them and leaving them with enough water to prolong dying for a day or two, or lashing them securely to a

125

fencepost close to a hill of hungry red ants. They saw no reason to exclude women and children from these pranks—the captured ones as victims, and their own as delighted spectators.

While I was reexploring the gory details of the Apache campaign, and refreshing my memory as to the ultimate fate of Geronimo, a friend brought me an old book long out of print. An outsized tome of about 550 pages, only part of which pertains to General Miles, it is a book I couldn't stop reading and now have read three times. Written in a flamboyant, dated style that defies all description, it is called *Deeds of Valor* and is a more or less official collection of accounts, as the title page has it, of "how American heroes won the Medal of Honor" between 1861 and 1903. On the crowded title page are the lines: "From records in the archives of the U.S. government," and "From personal reminiscences of officers and enlisted men. . . ." Books like this are now almost extinct, due to the scientific "weeding" programs of all the public libraries during the past twenty-five years.

Nobody could ever accuse the authors of *Deeds of Valor* of not knowing how to write. Even after reading only the preface. Just a few sample lines, and please take a deep breath:

> Let us nourish our patriotic enthusiasm, increase our strength, heat to an all-melting intensity the flame of our devotion by learning and imitating these examples of our fathers and forefathers. Aye, is there a nation, has there ever been a nation on this blessed globe whose history is more densely filled with heroic, astonishingly heroic deeds of a brighter lustre, than our own native American history.

Aye, there's *writing* for you. And the preface ends modestly:

> . . . this book certainly represents a publication both highly patriotic and unique, and, as to painstaking care and accuracy, unequalled by anything yet launched upon the market of Amer-

126

ican literature. As to those critics who seek fame in deriding the self-sacrificing loyalty of our national heroes we declare in the words of the Greek philosopher: "And if thou gnaw me to the root I shall bear fruit in spite of thee."

Quaint though it may sound to our ears, this book shows unmistakably just who were the popular national heroes of the early 1900's. A list of those described begins with admirals Schley and Dewey, then Miles, in that order, and includes Buffalo Bill Cody and General Arthur MacArthur, father of Douglas MacArthur. After the Wolf Mountain fight, no less than 31 of Miles' men were awarded the Medal of Honor. A large part of the book deals with the Indian campaigns, and Miles is mentioned more often than any other commander, in chapters with titles like "Through Texas with General Miles" and "Snatched from a Horrible Fate."

It is quite plain that some of the text, and much of the lore pertaining to Indians, was cribbed from Miles' *Recollections,* written a few years earlier. And much is made of the concept that the Indians were always driven to take the warpath only because of unbearable cruelties and all sorts of wrongs imposed on them by the whites.

Without this book, which contains an official list of all Medal of Honor winners, I might never have realized that Miles was responsible, in large part at least, for the practice of recommending Indian scouts for the award as well as regular Army men. On the list we find the names Achesay, Chiquito, Co-Rux-Te-Chod-Ish (Mad Bear), Elsatsoosu, Jim, Kohosa, Nannasaddie, Nantaje, and Rowdy. However, none of the exploits of these Indians is mentioned in the text. And this, it may be guessed, is because the book constantly promotes a popular fallacy of the times—that all Indians were treacherous, depraved savages, as in fact a few Apaches and others had become. It was by enlarging on this idea that the acts of heroism of the soldiers could be most enhanced.

The more fiendish the enemy, the more heroic the soldiers.

Another universally popular concept reflected was the belief that the Indians were not the victims of the white race itself, but only of certain white individuals. While granting that the Indians had been degraded and forced into fighting by the white man's injustices, those injustices were always represented as the acts of certain "bad" people—corrupt Indian agents or traders, some especially brutal Army officer, or Washington politicians. Nobody was ready to accept what Miles knew so well, that basically it was the great Western development and expansion itself which doomed the Indians to become a dwindling, disinherited minority with a vanishing culture; a people with hardly a better chance for survival than the buffalo.

In short, the Indian culture could not have long existed side by side with the enormously more populous white culture, even had the treaties been respected and the Indian affairs agents been more scrupulous. Miles was always trying to explain this to the enlightened leaders of the Indians, hoping to prevent them from the futility of attempting to win back their rights by fighting.

Strangely, it was the lowest level of writing at this time which came closest to reality. In the dime novels, almost universally banned to children in respectable homes, the Indians were probably described more accurately than in any other writings of the whole period. And something like 50 percent of the annual flood of dime novels were Indian-fighting stories of one sort or another.

Every kid who was not a hopeless sissy had a stack of these books hidden some place. In my own case, I had the good fortune to have a literary-minded grandfather with highly unorthodox tastes. He kept me supplied with dime novels, such as the Kit Carson series, in spite of my mother's protests that they were all trash. I knew all about the difference between good Indians and bad Indians; the Utes lived on grasshoppers, the Sioux on rare buffalo steaks; beautiful squaws made far better wives than any white women ever could. Indians were *people,* just as we were ourselves; not the noble savages or the depraved fiends so eloquently described in the pages of *Century* magazine.

Deeds of Valor contains one chapter very different in style from the others. It is the first-hand account of a cavalry unit's three-month chase of Apaches under the renegade chiefs Geronimo and Natchez, some two hundred miles down into Mexico and back, just before Miles took over the Arizona command from Crook. The writer, Marion P. Maus, was a lieutenant at the time. His commanding officer, Captain Crawford, was killed during the march, and Maus led his men back under incredible hardships. For a time he even had Geronimo and Natchez persuaded that their best course was to surrender, but they later changed their minds and escaped. Miles was so impressed with Maus' ability that he made the lieutenant his personal aide, a relationship that lasted many years.

Miles arrived in the Southwest in April, 1886, to replace Crook, who had been on the job for a number of years. Crook felt he had done well in keeping the Apaches on the run and claimed if he had been left alone he could have defeated them permanently in the near future. Miles, on the other hand, was of the opinion that Crook had wasted eight years without accomplishing much, and that with both Geronimo and Natchez still out, it might take years more to end the Apache raids and atrocities, unless very drastic changes were made in the Army's tactics. Crook believed that troops could not fight the Apaches effectively on their own terms; he had relied on large bands of hired Apache scouts to help defeat their own people. These scouts were always difficult to control and often unreliable.

Miles always believed in the judicious use of scouts, but never to do his fighting for him. And he was sure that if the troops were properly equipped and trained, and led by officers of his own selection, they could end the Apache threat forever in something like a year's time. How this turned out is summarized by Maus' journal, better, perhaps, than by a hundred and one other accounts I've read, or any efforts of my own. So I quote the piece, "Chasing Geronimo and Natchez," in full.

The surrender of Geronimo and Natchez, the leading chiefs of the Apaches, concluded the campaign of 1886. It marked the closing of a long and tedious war with the Apaches who had terrorized the whole southern part of Arizona and northern part of Mexico, and restored peace and prosperity to the inhabitants of a vast stretch of territory of two republics. Of all Indian savages the Apache is known to be most brutal, unruly, and barbarous. His treachery is proverbial, his cruelty notorious.

The young Apache warrior could not hope to command the respect of his tribe unless he had accomplished a "heroic" deed. This consisted of an outrage upon some hostile Indian, an American or Mexican ranchman, or a lone traveler. The more cruel the act, the greater the "heroism"; the more "heroic" deeds, the greater the honor and respect among his own people.

This principle inculcated in the child, actuated the youthful warrior and was practiced by the old and experienced. It made the Apaches the most dreaded and feared of all Indians.

In 1886 General Miles was called upon to subdue these turbulent and desperate bands and restore order in the territory mentioned.

The mountainous character of the country furnished these murderous savages with innumerable places of hiding and refuge and rendered them extremely difficult to get at. Many expeditions and campaigns had been previously undertaken and failed before the seemingly insurmountable obstacles. In preparing for his campaign General Miles was determined to chase and hound these hostiles and keep chasing and hounding them and not let up on them until sheer exhaustion should force them into final subjection.

It was to be a war to the finish between the white man's perseverance and endurance and the same qualities of the redskin, the outcome of which, General Miles figured, would inevitably be in favor of the better equipped and infinitely more intelligent white man.

There was not the slightest doubt in General Miles' mind that the Apaches could be subdued, and in assuming the command of the Department of Arizona he selected such officers for the discharge of important missions and duties as agreed with him on the general proposition and were sufficiently energetic to carry out the common idea.

Then the general formulated a definite and systematic plan of campaign, reorganized the troops, restored the confidence of the men, infused new hope into the minds of the timid ranchers and brought order out of chaos.

For the first time in the history of American military operations General Miles during this year made use of the heliostat and adopted the system of heliographic messages—signaling by mirrors—for the transmission of orders and reports of the movements of the hostile Indians.

Experiments with this system, invented by an English officer some twenty years before, had been previously made by American generals, but it was not finally adopted and practically used until General Miles conducted his Apache campaign in 1886. Stations were established on the highest peaks of the mountains all over the country. Thus the movements of the savages were kept under observation constantly, and much time, money and labor were saved in unnecessary and long and tedious marches in search of the elusive enemy. One more word about the Apaches. General Miles described them as follows:

"They were vicious and outlaws of the worst class. They were clad in such a way as to disguise themselves as much as possible. Masses of grass, bunches of weeds, twigs or small boughs were fastened under their hat bands very profusely, and also upon their shoulders and backs. Their clothing was trimmed in such a way that when lying upon the ground in a bunch of grass or at the head of a ravine, it was almost impossible to discover them. It was in this way that they were wont to commit their worst crimes. An unsuspecting ranchman or miner going along a road or trail would pass within a few feet of these concealed Apaches, and the first intimation he would have of their presence would be a bullet through his heart or brain."

The campaign began in the latter part of April. The Apaches themselves made the first move. They boldly left the mountain fastnesses of the Sierra Madres and came down upon the terror-stricken people of Northern Mexico. Among the first outrages committed was that of which the Peck family became victims. The sad story is told by Captain Leonard Wood, assistant surgeon, United States Army, in short but graphic words as follows:

"Peck's ranch was surrounded by Indians, the entire family was captured, and several of the farm-hands were killed. The husband was tied up and compelled to witness indescribable tortures inflicted upon his wife until she died. The terrible ordeal rendered him temporarily insane and as the Apaches, like most Indians, stand in awe of an insane person, they set him free as soon as they discovered his mental condition; otherwise he would never have been allowed to live. He was afterward found by his friends wandering about the place."

The family had two daughters, one of whom was outraged and shared the fate of her mother; the other, a little girl of ten years, was dragged upon the back of a horse and carried away into captivity. She was recaptured. On their flight through Mexican territory the Apaches met a force of seventy Mexicans. A volley was fired, killing an Indian woman, and the Indian who carried the child was wounded. This Indian's horse was shot at the same time. The little girl bravely ran away from her savage captor and was picked up by the jubilant Mexicans. The Indian ran towards the rocks and there stood off the entire Mexican force, killing seven of them, each of whom was shot through the head. He then made his escape.

On another occasion the hordes rode through a wood chopper's camp and killed seven white men. Another time they crept stealthily into a small creek and murdered five Mexican placer miners.

Many other instances of the most reckless brutality and cruelty marked the opening of this campaign.

The command which was selected by General Miles for the expedition was placed in charge of Captain Henry W. Lawton, Fourth United States Cavalry, and composed of the best officers and men available. Troops were frequently changed and provisions made for fresh transports to replace the tired and worn-out horses and pack-mules.

The pursuit of the Indians was now taken up and continued

with untiring perseverance. Over prairies, mountains, through valleys, across streams and thundering rapids, now about the peaks of giant mountains, now way down through canyons steep and narrow, wherever the trail of the Indians led the command followed. The Indians would pass straight over the highest ranges of the roughest mountains, abandon their horses and descend to the valleys below, where they would supply themselves with fresh animals by stealing them; the soldiers would send their horses around the impassable heights, climb the ascent on foot and slide down the descent. They would suffer from cold on the peaks and from an almost intolerable heat in the depths of the canyons. On one occasion the command marched twenty-six hours without a halt and was without water for eighteen hours in the intense heat of that season. The Indians were being driven from one place to another, from Arizona to Mexico, with the tenacious troops clinging to their heels.

There was an agreement with the Mexican Republic and the government in Washington by virtue of which United States troops could enter Mexican territory when in pursuit of hostile Indians, so that in this campaign the boundary line between the two countries created no obstacles.

Several times the Indians were brought to bay and forced to fight, for example, in the Pinito Mountains, in Sonora, May 3, 1886, where in the midst of the battle Lieutenant Powhatan H. Clark, Tenth United States Cavalry, dashed among the howling Apaches and at the peril of his life snatched from them a corporal who had been wounded and fallen into their hands.

This dash was made well in advance of the rest of the troopers, who were themselves so busily engaged in keeping the hostiles at bay that they had not noticed his absence. Clark's intrepidity and exceptional courage displayed by dashing among the savages, firing as he advanced and killing several of the hostiles before he reached the place where the corporal was lying, prevented the massacre of the man before the eyes of his comrades.

The hostiles were badly defeated. Again twelve days later at Santa Cruz, Sonora, another engagement took place in which Sergeant Samuel H. Craig, of the Fourth Cavalry, was severely wounded, but nevertheless fought in the front ranks of the troops and with blood-covered face led a most gallant charge.

The Indians were compelled to flee for their lives and leave their entire camp in the hands of the troops.

For three long months this inexorable chase was kept up until on July 13th the last and decisive blow was struck on the Yaqui River in Sonora in a section of the country that was almost impassable for man or beast.

Geronimo and Natchez evidently considered themselves safe from all attack, but Captain Lawton, by skillful manoeuvering, managed to surprise the whole camp and seize everything in sight, the Indians themselves having a very narrow escape from capture.

The savages now had tired of being the hunted game of the United States soldiers and yearned for peace. Geronimo especially was willing to submit to the inevitable and sent two of his women to open negotiations. He agreed to an unconditional surrender, begging only that he and his followers' lives be spared. This was promised. And thus Geronimo, the dreaded Apache chief, became a prisoner. He remained loyal, too, for when on the return march the command met a large Mexican force, which assumed a threatening attitude, and could have rendered the situation critical enough to make the outcome doubtful, Geronimo and his Apaches stuck to the command, and so eager were they to assist those to whom they had surrendered only a short time before that a clash between them and the Mexicans was but narrowly avoided. On September 3rd Geronimo surrendered to General Miles in person at Skeleton Canyon, whither the commander of the campaign had ridden with another of his units on a rapid march to join Captain Lawton.

Natchez still refused to come in, but General Miles brought about his surrender by a stroke of clever diplomacy, which had worked wonders on a former occasion.

He overawed Geronimo with the marvels of the white man's civilization. Among other things he showed him the heliostat and explained that by means of this instrument he could talk and receive information at once from hundreds of miles away.

At the request of the superstitious Indian warrior the general inquired concerning the health of a brother of Geronimo, who was being held captive at a distant military post.

When the chief was given the news he had asked for he was

134

more terror-stricken than surprised, and sent a messenger to Natchez urging him to surrender, "as the white man was in league with powers strange and weird, and which he was not able to understand." A magic against which even the bravest Apache warriors could have no chance.

Natchez, perhaps glad to have a pretext to give up the hopeless and unequal struggle, followed the advice and surrendered on the same terms as Geronimo. His capture ended the Apache War.

15

---◆◄●►◆---

AS always, Miles continued his habit of scribbling a note to
Mary every night before going to sleep, though at times
while directing the chase of the Apaches he would be out
where there was no way to send mail for weeks at a time. Only
in this way could a man of such great natural reticence, when
it came to personal thoughts and emotions, find some freedom
of expression.

I have picked out a few letters which seem especially to
point up the nature of the Apache campaign and Miles' own
private thoughts about it.

> Fort Bowie
> Arizona Territory
> April 11 1886

Dear Mary,

I arrived today after a long, hot and very dusty trip. I think
this is the most barren region I have ever seen.

From what I can see and hear of the troops, they are very
much discouraged by being kept in the field so long and by the
prospect that the campaign must be continued for some time to
come. General Crook leaves tomorrow. He appears to feel very
much disappointed but does not say much. He tells me that only
two of the Apache warriors have been killed since they broke
out.

In many respects this is the most difficult task I have ever undertaken, on account of the extensive country, the natural difficulties and the fact that the hostiles are so few in number and yet so active. Still I can only make the best effort possible.

The letters always ended with some affectionate phrase, such as, "Your ever loving but lonesome husband, Nelson."

Nogales
May 8

Dear Mary,

This has been quite an anxious day with me, for I have been much annoyed with reports of Indians moving north. I have received telegraphic reports tonight, however, that are more favorable. It will take much time to organize fully such an extensive command and occupy such a vast territory. A more demoralized and inefficient command I have never known.

As soon as I can get away I want to go to New Mexico to make a thorough examination of the country and to systematize matters on that line [of outposts.]

Fort Huachuca
May 17

Dear Mary,

The Governor of Sonora came up to meet me here today. We have a good understanding and are working together. Our troops and the Mexicans have fought the Apaches five times in about ten days. There will be no let up of effort.

The Indians have enough ammunition [it is known] to last them five years, upwards of one hundred thousand rounds.

I have been constantly on the move. The reports of Indians in different places has made it necessary for me to be on several fronts. Thus far we have succeeded in keeping them out of our own country, with one exception. They came in west of Nogales and raided some ten or twelve miles along the border. The troops have been very active and have done good service.

Hatfield's command was not hurt seriously. He captured Geronimo's camp and some twenty head of stock. After that, in a fight, his horses got stampeded and he thought he had lost them, but he has recovered all but two.

It has been a busy and anxious day. I have heard of another fight. Lieutenant Brown got on to the Apaches and surprised them, capturing many arms, saddles, camp property and ammunition. From last reports they were much broken down, but the fiends recoup readily and I must give them no rest. I don't get much myself, I must say.

> Wilcox, Arizona
> May 30

Dear Mary,

This has been a very quiet Sunday and rather lonely one. This is a miserable little collection of mud and small buildings, about like Hays City or some of those western towns years ago, very hot and very dusty when the wind blows. The people, what few there are, are mostly cowboys and saloon keepers.

I am somewhat annoyed with official matters and the difficulties to be overcome. The condition of affairs was so bad when I came here that it is difficult to get things straightened out and confidence restored. Many of the troops have been in the field a whole year. Some are discouraged and to some extent demoralized; but I think matters will come out all right in the end. Several men have been killed and undoubtedly many others will be before the end is reached.

> Wilcox
> May 25

Dear Mary,

I am anxiously waiting to hear from different officers in charge of the troops. There is a band of Indians near the Apache agency, and I am anxious to know whether they can be made to surrender or whether they will turn back south again and continue hostilities. If they do, the campaign may last much longer. It is tiresome work and very difficult, but not more so than some other undertakings.

138

If the papers had not so much to say about it, I would like it better. But the trouble is, this war has been going on so long—in fact, it has been a chronic condition for the last thirty years.

Tucson
June 11

Dear Mary,

The last report places the Indians well down in Old Mexico and going south to escape the troops. I will have a fresh command well equipped in a few days to follow without regard to distance, should they continue their journeying down in Sonora.

Fort Huachua
June 15

Dear Mary,

This is a very difficult undertaking and everyone is saying I cannot succeed. But it has been said before, and I have never doubted my ability to make this country untenable for the Indians. I have received the most cordial and zealous support from the troops. I came down here to reorganize a command to operate in old Mexico, under Col. Lawton, and to make some changes in the disposition of troops.

During the next three months, up to the end of the campaign, Miles wrote so often and at such length that to include his letters in full here would take too much space. A few excerpts however may add to the story.

I am somewhat annoyed by the newspapers publishing such absurd and false statements. . . . One would suppose by their accounts that the whole country was full of Indians and that there was an Apache behind every cactus bush. I am also annoyed by the statements thrown out by Crook. He made a dead failure of this, as he has of every other campaign.

You will have seen in the papers about Geronimo wanting to surrender already, etc. There is no truth in this report, and in fact nearly everything you see in these "Arizona dispatches" is made up out of nothing. The correspondents send anything for sensation, and seem not to care whether it be true or false.

Crook's policy was to treat those Indians at the Apache reservation more like conquerors than prisoners . . . allowed to retain all their arms, ammunition and stolen property . . . if that policy is continued, they will furnish warriors for the next twenty years, liable to break out and raid the settlements any time they go on a drunk.

Nearly every American expects war [with Mexico] and most desire it, strange as it may seem. Although it is only about twenty years since the Civil War closed and the thick dark mantle of mourning was spread over our entire land, in that brief time our people are again anxious for war. . . . The result would undoubtedly be that Mexico would be absorbed. . . . I am not sure that our country would be any better off, and it might not be as well off.

I go down this morning (Sept. 2) to see the hostiles under Geronimo. They have said they wanted to see me. I have very little faith in their sincerity and do not anticipate any good results. But still there is one chance that they may come in, and I feel like exhausting every effort to get them in without any more loss of life, if possible.

On September 5, Miles wrote Mary the news that the campaign was ended. The matter-of-factness and lack of any jubilant remarks was typical:

Dear Mary,
The last of the hostile Apaches surrendered yesterday at Skeleton Creek, named so because of the number of skeletons found

140

there, result of massacres of years ago. I left there this morning and after a ride of 65 miles arrived at this place (Fort Bowie, Arizona) bringing Geronimo, Natches, the hereditary chief of the Apaches, and three others. The remainder under charge of Lawton will be here in three days. All well. Love to Celia and Sherman.

Crook had been trying to subdue the Apaches for about eight years. Miles had done it in five months.

16

---◄◆►---

AFTER 1886, for the rest of Miles' public career, the newspapers were to have more and more to do with the image of the general in his later years, an image that would remain so firmly fixed it would not be questioned by most researchers, even to the present. In ten to fifteen years after Mergenthaler's invention of the linotype (originally "line-of-type") machine in 1885, the newspaper publishing business rapidly developed into its golden age of power. It would have no rivals until the advent of radio; and the near perfection of telegraphic and telephonic communications, plus railroad rapid delivery, gave the printed news a practically universal and almost all-powerful influence on public opinion. At the same time, the newly created news services, Associated Press and United Press, and the inception of chain ownerships, helped put the larger newspapers in positions of great wealth.

As in some of the other big businesses and the high finance of that period, corruption reached a magnitude far exceeding anything previously seen in this country. Among the publishing titans, competition was ruthless and savage. It has often been said that the Hearst papers alone actually caused the Spanish-American War by their sensational fabrications. If that is an exaggeration, most historians today agree that had the Hearst papers opposed the war, it might not have occurred. It naturally followed that the men who owned the larger newspapers were the peers of Presidents, Senators, captains of industry, and financiers. Hearst was in Congress himself for a time and was once nearly nominated for the Presidency.

There may have been a few other men of importance in those times who had no fear of newspapers. But Nelson A. Miles seems to have taken all the honors among military commanders for loudly damning the press whenever he disagreed with it, and to hell with the consequences. Nor had he ever gone out of his way to supply the correspondents with colorful stories when real news was scarce, in the manner of contemporaries such as Custer, Cody, and Crook.

If Miles had not gained a very strong position in the higher echelon of the Army before the newspapers became so powerful, they would have ruined him. As it was, some of them had a good try at it from time to time. After the successful termination of the Apache campaign of 1886, Miles wrote Mary that his chief reward from Washington was total silence. This was undoubtedly because the press had refused to play up his part in the victory, preferring instead to print the ready statements and comments of his unsuccessful predecessor, General Crook. Crook was still insisting that it was he who had really beaten the Apaches and that Miles had just appeared on the scene in the last act to try to garner all the credit.

Meanwhile Miles was embroiled as usual in all sorts of complicated dealings with the government in an effort to see justice done to the conquered Indians. He wanted to prevent a wholesale deportation of all Apaches to Florida, and above all, to see that the leaders were granted amnesty as defeated warriors and not turned over to civil courts as murderers. The affair dragged on for three or four years, but ultimately Miles was partially successful.

The General did, however, approve of the deportation to

Florida of all those Apaches who had been actively hostile and out on the warpath under Geronimo and Natchez. His reasoning was that if they were not moved quickly to a far-off section of the country, the desire for vengeance in the West would result in their being handed over to civil courts. He knew that court actions of the Southwest frontier in those days often turned out to be lynching parties, and were quite sure to be in the case of the hated Apaches.

Luckily Miles didn't wait for any further discussion of the matter by his superiors. He packed the hostiles into specially requisitioned trains as soon as they were rounded up and sent them on their way east. Meanwhile, President Harrison had been pressured by some Western Congressmen to send orders to Miles directing that the hostiles be turned over to the civil courts for trial. Miles wired the President that it was too late: the Apaches were already on their way to Florida, and furthermore, he was complying with the terms of their surrender which he had been authorized to guarantee them, insuring that they would be protected as prisoners of war and not tried for murder.

Harrison was furious. He liked to think of himself as a high-minded statesman who could never be accused of breaking a pledge to his supporters. Miles had placed him, perhaps inadvertently, in the position of having publicly agreed to something he couldn't very well carry out. Had he ordered that the Apaches be sent back from Florida, a messy business at best, Miles would be sure to accuse the Administration of having authorized terms of surrender which had been violated. All Harrison could do was to imply, without actually trying to prove it, that Miles had acted beyond his authority; and to hope the whole matter would quickly be forgotten.

The episode was probably one reason why, in 1888, it was Crook instead of Miles who was promoted to the major general's position opened by the retirement of Terry. Miles was then sent out to command the Division of the Pacific, but without promotion in rank, with headquarters in San Francisco. The Secretary of War wanted to keep him as far away from Washington politics as possible.

It was at about this time that Miles' Western friends first publicly suggested he should run for President. When his non-committal reply gave the impression that he might consider it, many Eastern papers came out with stories to the effect that he was using the publicity gained from the Indian campaigns to promote himself politically. But the New York *World,* followed by some of the smaller papers, came out in his defense.

Digging through the old files so long afterward, I was impressed by something that seems, to me at least, an ironic fact. The papers defending Miles, like those opposing him, always avoided for some reason ever picturing the kind of man he really was, and what he really stood for. Pondering this in retrospect, the reasons may now be fairly obvious. The General was hardly more cooperative with friendly papers than with unfriendly ones. He carried personal reticence to such lengths that even love letters to his wife sound as though they were designed to be read aloud at a Sunday school gathering. On the other hand, in any matter he considered to be in the public domain, such as a treaty between an Indian tribe and the government, he would be frank to the point of outspoken condemnation of a whole administration beginning with whoever happened to be President at the time.

At this point in his life it began to look as though this independent—some would say autocratic—self-educated Yankee would never learn just how much the world had changed during the twenty years he had been fighting Indians out in the wilds beyond the frontiers. Newspapers, as he had known them, were supposed to print the news. The idea never crossed his mind that the time had come when anyone in a position of importance must either play ball with the all-powerful

145

press or take the consequences. And a part of those consequences were that most historians, long afterward, would form
opinions largely shaped by studying old press files.

While in California Miles traveled all over the state and became chiefly interested in the potentials for irrigation on a
scale much larger than had ever been tried before. He wrote
a few articles, foreseeing the enormous agricultural development of the valleys which were later to become among the
world's greatest food-producing areas. In order to appreciate
his efforts along those lines, it should be remembered that,
at an even later date, most Californians still thought of their
state's productive future in terms of either mining or lumbering.

In the spring of 1890 Crook died suddenly of a heart attack.
Again Miles hoped to be named to fill the vacancy in the top
echelon of the Army. There was no higher rank at the time—
the commanding general of the Army, Schofield, was himself
ranked as a major general. The title of lieutenant general had
been discontinued and was not revived until after the Spanish-American War.

Miles seems to have been victimized rather than aided by
the influence of his wife's eminent relatives (some accusations
in the press to the contrary). This time it was Mary's Uncle
John Sherman, one of the most prominent U.S. Senators, who
advised Miles to stay away from Washington. The President,
the Senator said, was still angry at Miles because of the Apache
affair, and would certainly not make the necessary recommendation for a promotion. But Miles had finally learned not
to rely on anyone but himself. He disregarded Uncle John's
message and took the first train to the Capitol. There he managed to get an hour's private interview with the President.
What transpired was not recorded, but Miles emerged from
the White House with high expectations.

He told his mother-in-law, Mrs. Charles Sherman, who was

146

in Washington at the time, that he thought the interview had gone very well. He liked the President personally and felt that Harrison had become much more friendly after listening to an explanation in some detail of Miles' motives in past controversies concerning what was to be done with the Apache hostiles. Later that same day the recommendation for promotion was sent to the Congress and was immediately voted approval. Miles sent jubilant telegrams to his wife and daughter in San Francisco, adding the words Major General after his name.

The promotion involved a transfer to take over the command of the Division of the Missouri. This was the command including the Dakotas and Montana, where Miles had served under Terry and scored his great victory over the Sioux thirteen years earlier. That area had remained peaceful since Miles had left Montana, but now another great Sioux outbreak was in the making. This time Miles couldn't ride off into the wilderness at the head of his own handpicked regiment, as he had done so many times in the old days. No major general could think of proceeding directly to the scene of action, however much he might wish to. The job of running the whole vast division meant sticking close to headquarters, evaluating information, and delegating authority all the way down the chain of command.

There was no time for the inspection and training of specialized units, or the selection of officers, such as Miles had been able to do in former commands. Here he inherited the men and the officers who had been operating for years under Crook, and he would have to use them pretty much as he found them, for better or worse. Army regulations would not permit bringing in units and officers from other divisions. If action were to develop at any moment, which seemed likely, the best Miles could do was to employ some of the same scouts he had found so useful in the first Sioux campaign, including Buffalo Bill Cody.

Also totally different from the old days was the nature of this insurrection; it was so fantastically anachronistic that when the news of it burst on the country at large, most Easterners took for granted it must be largely an invention of the newspapers. But even the most sensational of reporters could hardly have embroidered any stranger stories than were contained in the official bulletins. The Sioux tribes, for years thought to be thoroughly pacified and domesticated, were leaving the reservations by the thousands and again preparing to go on the warpath. It did not seem possible at a time when their former hunting grounds in the Northwestern states had been crisscrossed with railroads and dotted with modern cities and towns, lighted by electricity and interlaced with telephone lines.

It had taken an occasional hardy correspondent several weeks by riverboat and horseback to reach the scene of the Custer massacre in 1877. Now hundreds of reporters rode on pullman cars close to the areas where action was expected and wrote their dispatches in the red-plush upholstered comfort of hotel rooms. Troops still had to patrol in large areas of wilderness, but problems of supply and communications were vastly easier than a few short years earlier.

The immediate cause of this uprising was a rapidly spreading wave of quasi-religious fanaticism among Indians all over the Northwest. This sudden and quite unprecedented movement was called the Ghost Dance, or just the Dancers. It was started by a self-styled Indian messiah in Idaho. He foretold that the day was almost at hand when all the Indians' ancient lands and freedoms would be restored to them. If they would band together in certain wilderness meeting places and dance with great energy and dedication, their warrior ancestors would return to earth and help them to victory.

It would take a great deal more space than a few pages to describe, in any detail, the complex events which had set the stage for a wholesale adoption of the cult. It was the old story of increasing mistreatment by the government since the first Sioux uprising thirteen years earlier. But this revolt had also been given great impetus by the misguided work of missionaries, societies set up to aid the Indians, and various Eastern liberals. The very people who had thought they had accomplished the permanent pacification of all the tribes had in fact made conditions intolerable for the Sioux.

Typical of those who thought they knew what was best for the Indians was Senator Henry L. Dawes, who stated publicly that if the Sioux were starving it was their own fault because they hadn't tended their farms industriously enough. He ignored the ruinous droughts of the past two seasons, among other factors. The Indians *were* starving. They had been coming closer to it year after year. Beef and other food rations allotted to the reservations by Congress never reached the intended beneficiaries. Almost invariably the agents in charge of reservations were political appointees who grafted unmercifully at their jobs.

The missionaries had been too concerned with trying to Christianize all the Indians to pay much attention to their material needs. And in the firm belief that hunting and the primitive ways of wilderness life were not conducive to religion, the missionaries also supported a plan to take away nearly all the Sioux hunting lands which had been legally ceded to them by the government. Nine million acres were seized and barred to the Indians in a single deal in 1889. The land commission that put through this gigantic steal was to pay the Indians a few millions (considerably less than a dollar an acre, even though some of the land was being farmed by Indians who had to abandon their homesteads and depart with whatever they could carry on their backs), and the money was to be used for food, more schools, roads, and other benefits. But somehow none of the payments ever reached the Indians. Actually, the transaction had never been agreed to by any of the responsible Indian leaders, but certain depraved or ignorant chiefs had been bribed to sign the deeds. The missionaries and many Eastern do-gooders even believed that by thus taking away the Indians' hunting grounds, they had helped their red brothers to become "civilized" more quickly.

17

THE bottom was reached in 1890, with more Indians actually starving than ever before in history. Every reservation by this time had a certain number of more or less educated families, people who had tried the ways of the white man but nevertheless saw their children dying before their eyes, one by one, from nothing more than malnutrition. The Sioux, try as they would, could not in one generation become farmers, and the two-year drought, with none of the promised government relief rations ever reaching them, reduced them to utter despair.

So, when the Idaho medicine man-prophet proclaimed the moment had arrived, they embraced the new mystical faith as an absolute last resort. They had tried everything else, and failed. Within a few months Ghost Dance ceremonies were being held in all the reservations of the Northwest. When alarmed authorities prohibited this heathen exhibition, the Indians went out into the wilderness and kept on with the dance. Meanwhile large supplies of arms and ammunition were being stockpiled by the younger and more militant of the Indian leaders. And the more fanatical of their followers had come to believe that they were immune to the white man's guns when they had donned the charmed shirts of the Ghost Dancers.

Among the more bizarre aspects of this last great Indian uprising was that the hostiles, as well as the soldiers, sometimes traveled by train. From reservations throughout the west, Indians who decided to join the Ghost Dancers would pack up their rifles, war paint, and fighting costumes in battered suitcases and head for the nearest railroad station. A day or two later they would get off at Pine Ridge reservation, a South Dakota rallying point, and disappear in the direction of the Bad Lands.

Among the Sioux who were fighting Custer in 1876 there were probably some who had never before laid eyes on white men. This time some of the hostiles had been East to the Carlisle School for Indians, and many had the rudiments of an education imparted by mission schools on the reservations. There were actually college graduates among the braves on the warpath. Unable to get good jobs, disillusioned at the appalling treatment of their kinfolk on the reservations (the term "concentration camp" hadn't been invented then), these young men had decided to revert to the ways of their fathers. This was too shocking to be readily believed by the Eastern liberals, the "Friends of the Indian" groups, all of whom firmly believed that enforced education must automatically solve all the Indians' problems and grievances.

In writing this, after some of the greatest and most disastrous race riots in American history, it is impossible to avoid at least a passing thought about the similarities in the thinking of those young Sioux belligerents, especially the educated ones who reverted to the desperate fanaticism of the Ghost Dance, and the present young Negroes of the Black Power group. Every Black Power slogan has had its almost identical counterpart, seventy-seven years ago, in the Ghost Dance movement. The objective was the same—to get what the white man's so-called laws had failed to provide, by killing, looting, destroying. Better to risk being killed by the soldiers than to tolerate any further injustice.

During the first few months of his new command, Miles

took pains to keep fully informed of the Ghost Dance movement; he foresaw, as no one in Washington did, the violence of the holocaust it might unleash. Orders were issued to break up all Ghost Dance conclaves, but existing reservation agencies were far too corrupt or inefficient to be able to accomplish this. The Army might have been able to do it, but it was not given enough authority by the federal government. Eastern liberals were now sure the Army was composed of a crowd of thugs who only wanted to beat up the noble savages. Apparently they could not grasp that only a few years earlier it had been the Army, notably Miles' commands, that had in fact been the *only* sensible and effective champion of Indian rights.

General Miles, from his division headquarters in Chicago (of all places) was now supposed to direct the military affairs of the whole vast Division of the Missouri where all this Sioux outbreak buildup was taking place—including the Dakotas, western Nebraska, Wyoming, Idaho, and Montana. For months he worked frantically and often furiously, trying in vain to persuade either the Administration or the Congress to empower the Army to take more preventive action before it was too late.

He had often tried to persuade the government to return the jurisdiction over all Indian reservations to the Army, which had been charged with this function earlier in the century. There can be no doubt that had this been done, the Indians would at least have been protected from many of the abuses that drove them to revolt. But the dual combination of (a) the corrupt politicians and Indian agents who had found the annual Indian relief appropriations an easy way to line their own pockets and (b) the influential "liberal" elements of the East, whose members had never seen an Indian reservation in their lives, proved far too powerful. Nothing was done.

Meanwhile some of the Eastern papers busily took up the line that Miles' efforts in Washington were just a publicity stunt to follow up another recent move to promote him as a Presidential candidate. At the time, Miles was much too occupied with the dangers of the Sioux situation to pay any attention to the charges. Toward the end of December the situation remained tense, but there had as yet been no actual shooting. In a letter to Mary, Miles confided that he now had some hope the potential conflict could be averted.

Miles was especially worried by news that his old adversary, Sitting Bull, had left his reservation. The chief had at first refused to join the Ghost Dancers; but as the movement became more general, he became persuaded. Taking 200 well-armed warriors with him, he set off to find the other chiefs who had gone out into the Bad Lands. Miles wrote Mary on December 19: "I was intensely anxious to know whether I would have to encounter Sitting Bull, or whether he could be arrested. I gave a very positive order to that effect, and directed the commanding officer to make it his special duty to secure his person. . . ."

What happened is described in the *Recollections.*

A few hours' delay would have been fatal, as Sitting Bull . . . had made preparation to leave that morning and join the great hostile camp which was then assembled in the Bad Lands, preparatory to their movement west. Major Fechet moved his command at night some thirty miles to the close proximity of Sitting Bull's camp, and sent his Indian police forward to arrest the great war chief. They proceeded to Sitting Bull's lodge and, entering it, informed him that he was a prisoner, and that he must go with them. He protested, but to no avail. They had taken but a few steps when he raised the warcry which aroused his followers, who rushed to his rescue. Then occurred a short, desperate combat, in which Sitting Bull and quite a number of his immediate followers were killed, as well as five of the friendly Indian police who had made the arrest. The remainder held their position until the prompt arrival of the troops, who dispersed the hostile Indians in every direction.

So the last real encounter of that great Indian chieftain was a tragedy in which he fell by the hands of men of his own race. He was the strongest type of the hostile Indian that this country has produced. His reputation had been made by courage, energy, and intense hostility to the white race in his early days. He had gradually risen to leadership until he became the great organizing or controlling spirit of the hostile elements. None of the other Indians possessed such power to draw and mold the hearts of his people to one purpose, and his fall appeared to be the death-knell of the Indian supremacy in that western country.

Two or three days after the unplanned and sordid killing of Sitting Bull, Miles wrote Mary again:

So far, no white man has been killed and actual war has not commenced. I have done everything in my power to prevent one, but at times it seems impossible. The administration and the Republican Party are making a fatal mistake in not confirming the treaty . . . made with the Sioux. We have taken away their land. . . . The Indians have been half fed or half starved. Neither I nor any other official can assure the Indians that they will receive anything different in the future. They say, and very justly, that they are tired of broken promises. . . . I see they are talking in Congress of disarming [all] the Indians. That has been done two or three times, and the citizens sell them arms again. If they were disarmed there are enough horse and cattle thieves around the reservations to steal the Indians blind in six months. There has been no branch of our government so corrupt and disgraceful to the Republic as that which has had the management of our Indian affairs. . . .

Still outside their reservations were a number of large bands of Indians, in all probably several thousand well-armed warriors. Miles' strategy was to put all the available troops out in the field, deployed near all known Indian encampments but not close enough to risk a clash. It was hoped that the Army's superiority in having field guns, and the fact that the soldiers were obviously well prepared for battle, would reveal to the Indian leaders the hopelessness of their position if they chose to fight. Reliable Indian scouts and Indian police were sent out to parley with the Ghost Dancers wherever they could be found, with orders to try to persuade them to turn back toward their reservations. And it was hoped that the start of severe winter cold and some snow would induce the hostiles to "come in" at least until spring.

The plan began to work. Ghost Dancers were starting to straggle in to various reservations. Then on December 28, Colonel Forsyth, with a battalion of the 7th Cavalry, Custer's old outfit, ran across the encampment of a band led by a chief named Big Foot. There were some 350 Indians, but only about 100 warriors; the rest were women, children, and old men. Forsyth had 470 troopers, and he surrounded the Indian camp. Chief Big Foot sent out word that he was ill with pneumonia and asked to be treated by the Army doctor. This request was granted and as it was nearly nightfall, it was agreed that a parley would take place next morning.

At daybreak the chief asked to be returned to his camp. While this was being done, Forsyth told the Indians they would have to give up all their arms, and ordered a detachment of troops to go into the camp to collect them. The Indians had apparently decided to allow the troops to escort them back to their reservation, but most refused to give up their guns, saying that without them they would be unable to kill any game, and as they had little other food they would soon be starving.

Forsyth then instructed the troops to take the guns anyway, and as they started searching the tepees a shot was fired, probably by some young Indian. The nervous troopers replied with a general fusillade, and as one survivor described it afterward, in a few seconds all hell had broken loose. Forsyth then called in all the surrounding troopers and opened up with his field guns, and the encampment was practically annihilated. It was estimated that almost 300 Indians were killed or fatally wounded; women, children, and even babies were indiscriminately butchered. But Forsyth's stupid action had also lost the troopers 25 dead and 35 wounded.

Almost at once news of this massacre began to reach other bands of Ghost Dancers on their way back to the reservations. Many took it as a sure sign the Army meant to trick them into the same fate that had befallen Big Foot and his followers. Better now to fight it out to the last man.

As for Forsyth, he came close to being wiped out with his whole command, in the manner of Custer. Ambushed while returning from Big Foot's encampment (later that action was known as the Battle of Wounded Knee, after the name of the creek where it took place), his force was surrounded by a much larger band of enraged hostiles seeking revenge. As the Indians were starting to attack, a strong force from another cavalry outfit fortunately happened to ride up and was able to drive them off. This was the more humiliating to Forsyth because his proud 7th Cavalry battalion had been saved by a colored unit—the 9th, under Col. Guy Henry.

When the dispatch giving the main facts of Forsyth's destruction of Big Foot's encampment at Wounded Knee reached Miles, it probably infuriated him more than anything else that had ever happened in his entire military career. Schofield, commanding general of the Army in Washington, on the other hand, received the same dispatch as though it were the best of good tidings. He sent a wire to Miles requesting that his appreciation be passed along to the 7th Cavalry for its "splendid conduct."

Miles sent back a terse answer to the effect that as he was ordering an investigation into the very grave matter of Colonel Forsyth's actions at Wounded Knee, perhaps Schofield would wish to postpone his congratulations. At this, Schofield went into a huddle with the Secretary of War and the President. The result was a message from the President himself to Miles directing that if any officer had committed any misconduct he should be relieved of his command. Miles took the message literally and promptly wrote an order suspending Forsyth. He then boarded the next train for Pine Ridge, the reservation nearest the Bad Lands, where he planned to take direct command.

More troops from all over the West were now being sent to the area by train. As fast as they arrived, Miles sent them out to preplanned stations in a vast square around the territory where most of the hostiles were still encamped or moving about. But every precaution was taken to prevent further actual contact with the Indians. Miles still hoped to be able to persuade them to surrender and return to the reservations instead of fighting it out.

Little action developed during the next two weeks, but Miles did not get much sleep. Once a battle was narrowly averted when an officer, sent out to parley with some Sioux chiefs under a flag of truce, was shot and killed as he started to return. (It was later verified that his assassin was a graduate of Carlisle who had become a fanatical convert to the Ghost Dance cause.)

Finally, quite suddenly, the Miles policy of persuasion and parley, backed by a show of great force held firmly in check, showed real signs of success. By January 15 the General was able to write his wife that practically all danger was past. The Indians, five to six thousand strong, were pouring into the agencies and scattered railroad stations, having been told by their principal leaders to return peaceably to their reservations. It was, in a way, a rather bitter triumph for Miles. He got no commendations from Washington for having ended the campaign with so little bloodshed. A surprisingly large number of both the military people and the general public still held it would have been better if the whole Army had closed in on the Indians and wiped them out.

The War Department was indignant at Miles' having suspended Forsyth instead of hushing up that affair at Wounded Knee. All of Miles' evidence was ignored; a special whitewash board of inquiry completely exonerated Forsyth and even found him deserving of official praise for unusual gallantry. As for all those slain women and children, the board decided in its just wisdom that most of them must have been hit by the fire from their own warriors.

As seen by a large portion of the press in the 1890's, the favorite heroes were those who fought the bloodiest battles; *avoiding* battles, however brilliantly and justifiably, was not the way to gain mass popularity. This fact of life would never have the slightest effect on the future behavior of Nelson A. Miles. He never missed a chance, after Forsyth had been reinstated, to announce as publicly and loudly as possible that the colonel of the 7th Cavalry had been guilty on every count.

There is reason to believe that had not Miles suspended Forsyth immediately after the Wounded Knee massacre, the Sioux would never have come in without a big fight. (Headlines thoughout the country had given sensational publicity to Miles' action against Forsyth.) A great number of lives could have been lost on both sides if fighting had continued. The factor which, more than anything else, led the Sioux chiefs finally to trust Miles was the knowledge that he had suspended Forsyth and determined that no action such as that of Wounded Knee would be repeated.

All this was far too involved to be of any interest to the War Department or to most of the American public. Miles was called a sorehead, and a coddler of murderous Indians. Many newspapers saw to it that he would be remembered more for his "persecution" of that brave Indian slayer, Forsyth, than for skillfully averting a major Indian war—a war that the disappointed correspondents had once happily predicted was inevitable.

18

———◄◄◆►►———

FOR the next six years, from 1892 to the spring of 1898, when war with Spain was declared, the kind of life led by Maj. Gen. Nelson A. Miles and his family was about as far removed as possible from all their earlier experiences together. It began with a transfer to the Division of the East, where the Mileses, who had spent so many years in quarters ranging from wilderness tenting grounds to, at best, the plain and unspacious cantonment homes the always impoverished Army provided for its officers, would find themselves suddenly catapulted into the elaborate, rich, and incredibly artificial (though often perfectly sincere) social worlds of New York and Washington. In time, they would also take in the capitals and courts of Europe.

For Mary, fortunately, it was a world she had known to a considerable extent as a girl, the Shermans having been prominent in both Ohio and Washington. For her the adjustment was easy. Less understandable is the fact that her husband, the self-educated son of a poor farm family of rural Massachusetts, the rugged professional soldier and longtime Indian fighter of the frontiers, seemed even more at home in the ornately formal social world of those days. Nevertheless, it is apparent that Nelson Miles was the sort of man who could walk into the most select Washington salon with the same assurance and dignity he had shown in the old West when riding into some wilderness conclave.

It was this unexpected talent for the social and diplomatic scene that led to Miles' being sent abroad by the President in 1897 as a military observer of European armies, and also as the U.S. military representative at Queen Victoria's jubilee. Of course those newspapers which disliked him came out with stories that the Administration had sent him abroad to keep him away from the political front. There seems to have been no real basis for such conjecture. But it is interesting to note that writers of recent years who have mentioned this period in Miles' career have repeated that old bit of gossip as if it were a recorded fact.

During those years, two events brought him a good deal of national publicity. The first was his directing of the troops, by order of President Cleveland, in suppressing the great Chicago labor riots of 1894. The second was his appointment as commanding general of the U.S. Army in 1895, when Schofield retired.

In the 1890's all labor riots and most other subversive activities were said to have been inspired by "anarchists." These characters were sometimes real, sometimes falsely labeled, and often entirely imaginary. But all too real was the growing menace of the riots.

A few of the genuine anarchists, as distinguished from the many labor organizers often wrongly accused as such, had selected Chicago as the best base for launching their movement to overthrow the U.S. government by force. The rapidly growing metropolis, by now internationally known for its lawlessness, embodied the greatest extremes of wealth and poverty. Meat packers and farm machinery works were repeatedly harassed by violent strikes, some of which were in fact promoted by anarchists under the pretense of aiding the laborers. Notable among the more active of the rabble-rousers were a daughter of Karl Marx and her husband.

In the Haymarket riots of 1886, a bombing had caused the deaths of several policemen and wounded dozens more. The affair had led to a final conviction, for murder, of four labor leaders; two others also condemned to hang had been given last-minute commutations to life imprisonment. The Haymarket convictions had quieted things down only temporarily; by 1894 the labor union forces were ready to go into action again. This time the chief target was the Pullman Car Company, which involved a general strike against all the railroads in the Chicago area. A dangerous food shortage was soon brought on throughout the central part of the country. In July the strike got entirely out of hand, so far as the police were concerned, and mobs started looting and burning in several of the more depressed sections of the city.

Miles was called to Washington by President Cleveland for an emergency meeting. It was decided that Cleveland would order federal troops into the area to quell the disturbance. Commanding General of the Army Schofield, who was at the meeting, was apparently happy to let Miles direct the whole operation; he probably foresaw a nasty, thankless job not likely to cast much glory on his possible successor.

For the most part, that was how it turned out. Miles rushed to Chicago and began deploying the troops as they arrived, dashing about the city, day and night, as though it were a Sioux battlefield in Montana. The men had the strictest orders not to shoot. Miles was determined there would be no bloodshed unless the mobs broke through his lines and started attacking public buildings. For two weeks the outcome was uncertain, with a good deal of rioting still going on in some confined areas, but the troops did not have to resort to any actual shooting. By July 18, peace had been restored to all parts of the city, and Miles was able to withdraw all the federal forces soon afterward.

When it was assured that the trouble had been ended, Schofield let it be known that he was "displeased" with Miles' handling of the troops, but without mentioning anything specific enough to sound very convincing. The liberals and leftists quite naturally held up Miles as a symbol of military oppression and brutality, rather than seeing him as an officer who was forced to carry out, by order of the President, an assignment which would have resulted in much bloodshed had it been in any way bungled. At the same time, the conservative elements, the capitalists and antilabor people, accused Miles of being too lenient. He had let them down by not shooting a number of those miserable strikers when he had had a good chance. Such critics were not any happier when Miles stated publicly that he was fully in sympathy with labor unions, and even strikes, so long as no violence or lawlessness was tolerated.

Fortunately for Miles, the affair was pretty well forgotten by the time Schofield retired the next year. And furthermore, nobody really cared who would be named to command the Army. In 1895 the entire military personnel still numbered only 25,000, with some ten brigadier generals and five major generals. (In 1967 more than a million *civilians* were employed by the Department of Defense.) It was said that promotions were so slow there were many West Point-trained second lieutenants with grown-up grandchildren. Even such a tiny army was thought to be unnecessary by most Americans, now that the Indian wars were ended. This opinion was reflected in Congress by the woefully inadequate funds annually appropriated to support the military.

Even though it went largely unnoticed by the rest of the population, the appointment of Nelson A. Miles as commander of the U.S. Army was an occasion for rejoicing to the General and his family that nothing else could ever equal. This was the top, the end of the long climb. There wasn't anywhere higher to go. Except, of course, the Presidency—but Miles, the dedicated career Army man, would never have thought of that possibility, except for the sincere suggestion of the idea by some of his friends and admirers. He was not a man to balk at such a suggestion, but there is no evidence that he ever actually tried very hard to promote himself for the nomination. Nor did he ever approach politics with anything like the interest and energy he put into advancing his military career.

What did occupy Miles' vast energies much of the time for the next two or three years was an all-out effort to get a larger Army appropriation from Congress. He developed a detailed plan for raising the permanent peacetime Army strength to 70,000. This was the absolute minimum necessary for the adequate defense of the territorial United States, he argued, with a logic which a few years later it would seem utterly ridiculous to ignore. But it must be admitted that the General's only talent for lobbying was his stubborn persistence. He failed to get anywhere at all in promoting his plan, either with Congress or with the Administration. The Army remained at 25,000 men, and military pay remained at subsistence levels.

Even a major general's salary was hardly enough to maintain anything but the most modest scale of living. But at about this time the Miles fortunes improved considerably. The General's father-in-law, Charles Sherman, had become a successful railroad magnate, and Mary came into a fair inheritance. Added to this, Miles had made some successful investments. On taking over the formal duties of commanding general in Washington, the Mileses were able to take up residence in quite an impressive and luxurious town house, with the servants necessary to entertain on a par with the top dignitaries of the government. Many of the illustrious Civil War generals, Grant among them, were never to escape financial difficulties; Miles had finally managed to become comfortably well off, and for the rest of his life he would remain so.

Much has been made of the legend that Miles was notoriously troublesome to one Washington Administration after another. Nearly everyone who has written anything about this aspect of his career has repeated such terms as "trouble-maker," "meddler in politics," "arrogant proclaimer of his own opinions," "self-righteous critic," and so on. Most of this seems directly traceable back to the powerful Hearst and Pulitzer presses of the nineties, with which he was extremely unpopular.

The fact is, Miles got along very well with the Cleveland Administration. Had he not, Cleveland would never have named him for the post of general of the army when Schofield retired. Cleveland had good reason to admire Miles' success in handling the Chicago riot crisis. If anything had gone drastically wrong in that operation, it would have seriously damaged the President's political standing. Cleveland retired from public life when his second term expired in 1896. The election in that year of the Republican candidate, William McKinley, portended little good for the future career of Nelson A. Miles or, in some ways, for the nation itself.

However, McKinley's first major decision relating to his highest ranking general was a happy one. He sent Miles abroad as a military observer of the current war between those ever chronic enemies, Turkey and Greece. Miles was also to act as a goodwill emissary to other European countries, including England, France, Germany, Italy, and Russia.

Any detailed travelogue about this extended tour would prove something of a bore, I'm sure, to present-day readers, completely fascinating though it all was to the Mileses. To them, ocean liners and railroad parlor-cars were the ultimate marvels of the modern world. Mary wrote the children frequent long accounts of the trip. Sherman was then attending a Friends preparatory school. Cecelia, twenty-seven and not yet married, stayed in Washington to look after her young brother and manage the household. It is said that Cecelia was also very active in social affairs, and quite a sought-after belle about town until her marriage three years later.

Even Miles' most biased critics could not deny that he was eminently successful as a roving ambassador and expert observer of foreign armies. Always an enthusiastic traveler and tireless sightseer, he was an amateur anthropologist with interests ranging from archaeology to the possible future application of horseless carriages to military use. Nothing American had ever caught the imaginations of Europeans generally so much as Indian fighting and the frontier life of the American West, and Miles' reputation was much more glamorized abroad than at home. He was royally received and entertained in one capital after another.

By the end of the elaborate goings-on of the Queen Victoria's jubilee in London, where the Mileses were presented at court and had to attend many other state occasions, Mary was exhausted and showing signs of some minor illness. The General left her taking the waters at one of those German spas which, in those days, were thought to cure their clients of whatever might be ailing them, and went dashing off to visit the Czar in St. Petersburg and have a look at the Russian armies. When he returned, Mary was feeling quite recovered, and they set out for home with the feeling of embarking on something of a triumphal voyage. But it turned out the Administration had lost all interest in Miles' observations abroad.

The Mileses landed in New York to find the country at large—the press, the Congress, the Administration, the hack drivers, the bellhops, or whoever—all excited about a possible war with Spain. Of all countries in the world the United States could have chosen for its first foreign adversary since independence, Spain! On his trip to observe the "important" armies of Europe, Miles had not been instructed to bother with Spain at all.

At that time, most Americans still thought the situation implied merely a possible "Cuban" war. Just sending a few troops down to a little island only 90 miles from Florida (and many Americans didn't even know exactly where Florida was, in those pre-Miami days) to liberate the poor downtrodden Cuban patriots from their sadistic and imperialistic Spanish governors. As for how and why the Philippine Islands, halfway around the world, should become in any way involved in this Cuban business is a matter which I admit has mystified me in our time almost as much as it did General Miles in 1898.

The national preoccupation with Spain was most unfortunate, not only for Miles himself at the time—the effect being to create a total lack of interest, on the part of the press and Washington, in the results and conclusions of his foreign travels—but it had also the lasting effect of obscuring, even to the present time, an important historical fact of Miles' official career. Even if he had never done anything else of special note, he should have been better remembered in our military history, for in well over a century, since the Revolution actually, no other commander of the U.S. Army had gone overseas to study and observe foreign armies and foreign lands and governments.

There are some interesting angles to this. On his return, Miles was the only important military man in the country who foresaw, and in fact predicted, that the German military establishment would probably cause a European war in a few years which might involve the United States. Hence his urgently renewed plea for a much larger Army and a much larger military appropriation for *defense* purposes. But the most intensified conviction Miles brought back after his foreign observations was that the United States must make every possible effort to avoid any military involvement outside its borders. His studies had resulted in a belief that wars of so-called "liberation" always became, in greater or lesser degree, wars of imperialistic aggression.

It must have seemed to Miles the irony of all ironies when Congress, within the year, did indeed raise more money at last

167

for the Army. Fifty million dollars more, in fact, after several years of futile requests by Miles for even a small fraction of such a sum. But, alas, this was not for defense—it was raised to support the sort of war outside our borders that Miles most feared and deplored; a war he thought avoidable and unjustified, but in which he would have to serve as commander-in-chief of the U.S. Army.

It would be nice to be able to make the claim that in 1898 many of our high-ranking military people were opposed to engaging in any war, not only on foreign shores but against an "enemy" which obviously had no thoughts of attacking the United States, and was in no position to do so. (As it would be nice if we could make a similar claim today with regard to the situation before it was decided to send an army to Vietnam.)

Unfortunately, the opposite was true. During the buildup for war in 1898, General Miles was the only prominent active military man to raise his voice against the jingoists, warmongers, and those sincere but misguided patriots who believed it was our Christian duty to send our armies abroad so that, by military conquest, we could set up successful "democracies" in our own image. The realistic Miles view was supported only by a small minority of intellectuals and so-called "liberals." His opinion was ignored by the Administration, just as in our time Gen. James M. Gavin's prudent advice and accurate predictions concerning Viet Nam were ignored by the Administration.

The popular tenor of thought sweeping the country was expressed by Senator Albert J. Beveridge of Indiana, who wrote:

> We will establish trading posts throughout the world as distributing points for American products. We will cover the ocean with our merchant marine. We will build a navy to the measure of our greatness. Great colonies governing themselves, flying our flag and trading with us, will grow about our posts of trade. Our institutions will follow our flag on the wings of our

commerce. And American laws will plant themselves on shores hitherto bloody and benighted, but by those agencies of God henceforth made beautiful and bright.

On first taking office, McKinley was definitely opposed to war. But when public opinion began to swing more and more in favor of war, he decided it would be politically expedient to climb on the bandwagon, taking advantage of the support he would get from the big Hearst and Pulitzer newspaper combines and from various prowar factions in Congress.

At this point McKinley and his Secretary of War, Russell A. Alger, would gladly have ousted Miles if they could have found any valid excuse for doing it. But Miles was not going to leave his post just because the country was about to engage in a war he regarded ill advised and unnecessary. At the same time he characteristically refused to stop making his views public. Perhaps McKinley reasoned that if Miles were forced out as commanding general he might become even more embarrassing to the Administration.

Alger was an old professional politician and one of McKinley's more favored stooges—thoroughly incompetent in military matters, with ethics which were, to say the least, extremely flexible. There was no General Staff in those days, and the chain of command nominally ran from President to Secretary of War to commander of the Army. But there was no existing regulation or act of Congress to prevent the Administration from bypassing the commanding general of the Army whenever it chose. Even before war was declared, it was plain that the strategy of McKinley and Alger would be to issue orders, whenever it was likely Miles would disagree with their contents, directly to the various generals ostensibly under Miles' command.

Of course, whenever anything went wrong, the President let the blame rest on Miles as commander of the Army. It would be hard to imagine a more impossible position from which a military commander-in-chief would find himself trying to effectively direct the preparation for a war. He was forced to try to carry out unworkable orders from above, on the one hand. On the other hand, he frequently found his own orders to subordinates countermanded, several of the subordinate generals being in effect stooges appointed by the Administration.

In a recent book on current military affairs it was stated that the Pentagon spends $30,000,000 annually on public relations and publicity. In 1898 a public relations department for the Army had not been dreamed of, and there wasn't one dollar available for publicity. As commanding general, Miles considered it his duty to inform the public on all military matters. To the great annoyance of McKinley and Alger, he carried this policy to the extent of giving the press his own frank views on the impending war situation.

The prowar press and the proponents of war in Congress were demanding immediate invasion of Cuba. Miles declared that the Army was in no way adequate for such an invasion, and the necessary preparation would take many more months. Practical considerations aside, Miles claimed the war was being promoted on false grounds and its true objectives misrepresented to the public. Notable among those who shared Miles' views were former Presidents Harrison and Cleveland, but their opinions had little influence on the national level.

Miles had no effective support in Congress and none within the Administration, though at the outset certain cabinet members agreed with him, including his uncle-in-law, Secretary of State John Sherman. But John Sherman was growing senile to the point of being incompetent; and, in any case, McKinley wasn't interested in the views of his cabinet members.

As a one-man publicity department for the Army, Miles had very little success. Even some of his friends and others who sympathized with his opinions thought he was stepping outside his proper province as Army commander. But the General's pioneering in the complex realms of military publicity did have one lasting result—a rapid accumulation of more personal enemies than any other wartime commander-in-chief in our military history. Here is another likely clue to his subsequent disappearance from the ranks of our legendary Army heroes.

19

————◆◄◎►◆————

MANY factors leading up to the war with Spain were not generally known and not explained until years afterward, and indeed many still cause considerable argument. When, after World War I, historians and writers began to rediscover the Spanish-American War, a new slant on the whole affair was initiated which has been widely followed ever since. The theory was that the Hearst papers had been the chief cause of the war.

By this time Hearst himself was a benign, retired ancient; his newspaper empire was losing its great power, and the ruthlessness of the "yellow journals" was largely a thing of the past. It had become safe for the historian to blame all the jingoism and warmongering of 1898 on the Hearst papers.

On the other hand, the Pulitzer press, which had been equally active and unprincipled in promoting the war, had over the years acquired a reputation of great respectability. The famous Pulitzer Prizes were a national institution, and the unsavory past was conveniently forgotten. And so I have found that among recent books discussing the origins of the Spanish-American War most stress the blame of the Hearst papers without similarly blaming the Pulitzer press.

A very different judgment was expressed in some detail by Oswald Garrison Villard in his autobiography. In 1897 Villard became editor-publisher of the New York *Evening Post*, probably the most reputable and influential liberal newspaper in the United States at the time. (The famous liberal magazine, the *Nation,* was under the same management in its best years.)

Villard inherited the *Post* from his father, Henry Villard, a railroad magnate who had married the daughter of the great Boston abolitionist and reformer, William Lloyd Garrison. Almost alone among the capitalists of his time, Henry Villard was a tireless promoter of such causes as the legalization of labor unions, woman suffrage, tariff reform, antitrust laws, and civil rights. Another member of this famous clan was Wendell Phillips Garrison, an editor of the *Post* and the *Nation.*

All this is mentioned merely to show that even though some may not agree with all of Villard's opinions, few writers of his time enjoyed greater respect for honesty and sincerity. In his book, *The Fighting Years,* discussing the buildup for the Spanish-American War, Villard wrote:

> . . . the threat of war with Spain, which we [the *Post* editors] were bound to oppose, was intensified by the blowing up of the *Maine* and then by the hostilities brought about by President McKinley's dishonest handling of the situation. We were naturally in favor of the Cuban demand for self-government, sympathized with the rebels, and severely criticized the Spanish offer of autonomy made in the fall of 1897, feeling certain that it "could prove only a mockery and a source of fresh disaster to the Cubans." On the other hand, we were under no illusions as to the insurgents, knew that most of the newspaper stories about them were fakes, and were quite prepared for the proof, furnished when we got into the war, that they were in no position to aid the United States forces.
>
> We stood with McKinley in his message to Congress of December, 1897, when he declared that forcible annexation was not to be thought of; that by our code of morality it would be criminal aggression: and we stuck to the position when McKinley abandoned it and seized the Philippines. But the influence of *The*

Evening Post in the days leading up to war was slight when compared to the orgy of lying and sensationalism indulged in by the yellow journalists of the day, with Hearst and Pulitzer setting the pace. I believe that those months of unbridled sensationalism and the throwing off of any pretense of journalistic responsibility to the public left permanent marks upon the entire American press. . . . Despite this lurid furor McKinley could have prevented war had he been sincere in his desire to do so. Yet to this day the myth appears in many histories and memoirs that the good and benign McKinley fought to keep us out of war until an overwhelming popular and congressional demand drove him into it.

Nothing could be further from the truth, which is that Spain had surrendered on nearly every point. . . .

In other words, the "overwhelming popular and congressional demand" for war was largely abetted by McKinley himself. He did this by carefully keeping it secret that he had received a dispatch from Spain informing him the Spanish government was surrendering its sovereignty in Cuba; and he kept this momentous news quiet, except for a couple of unimportant details, at the very time Congress was preparing to vote its declaration of war measure. As he well knew, the cause of "liberating the Cubans from the Spanish" had been the backbone of the arguments for war.

It was in 1938 that Villard wrote the lines quoted here concerning the repetition by historians and writers of the "myth" that McKinley was forced into asking Congress to declare war quite against his will and his desire. What has happened to that theory from 1938 to the present? Perhaps the best evidence is to be found in the success of Margaret Leech's *In the Days of McKinley*, published in 1959. This enormously detailed biography—600 oversized pages plus nearly a hundred pages of notes—has been widely praised by historians and was a Book-of-the-Month-Club selection.

This book, which is so largely a history of the war with

174

Spain, in treating the prelude to war makes the Hearst press the big villain. The liberal press is conveniently ignored, and hardly any of the great liberal writers and scholars of those times, opposed to the war and hence not supporters of McKinley, are even mentioned, let alone quoted. With reference to the sudden military appropriation by Congress of $50,000,-000, it is admitted that this appropriation had been in response to the President's request. But this statement is followed by many pages of elaborate explanation that McKinley had advocated these funds *solely for defense,* all the time hoping to avert war. (Miles for years had been unable to get Congress to raise military appropriations by even *one* million!) Whether or not McKinley really expected to avert war is, of course, still a matter of opinion. Such a tremendous increase in our military establishment was hardly justified on purely "defense" grounds, against an adversary who was notoriously weak at the time and posed no threat whatever against our own territories.

According to Villard, the whole key to the matter lay in the hands of Gen. Stewart L. Woodford, then U.S. minister to Spain. (At that time we didn't even dignify the importance of Spain by sending an emissary with the title of ambassador.) It was Woodford's job to try to persuade the Spanish government to agree to an armistice in the civil war long going on in Cuba, with a permanent autonomous government guaranteed to the rebels, along lines that were to be approved by, and more or less directed by, the United States in the role of mediator.

In this difficult task Woodford was finally successful. Spain agreed very substantially to all our terms, and Woodford sent his famous dispatch to McKinley. The minister said afterward it was the proudest and happiest moment of his life. He expected that when his message was received, McKinley would announce to the country at large that war had been averted.

Reminiscing years later, Woodford said wryly, "When I

175

sent that last cable to McKinley, I thought I should wake up next morning to find myself acclaimed all over the United States for having achieved the greatest diplomatic victory in our history. . . . I heard only that the President would lay the matter before Congress—without a word of personal congratulation. The next thing I knew he went before Congress, failed to tell it all I had accomplished, and practically asked for the declaration of hostilities." Woodford did not realize that by the time he had effected the Spanish capitulation with regard to Cuba, the President had gone so far along the road toward war he was in no mind to back out.

Beginning about three months before his final message to Congress asking for a declaration of war, McKinley kept up a steady barrage of public statements to the effect that he was doing everything possible to prevent an armed conflict. The yellow journalists kept up a steady attack on his "cowardly" position, but McKinley knew he could afford to preserve his image as the humanitarian war-hating President. His Assistant Secretary of the Navy, Theodore Roosevelt, was meanwhile making all the noise necessary to promote war, aided by many other of McKinley's supporters in Congress. And in private, McKinley was seeing to it that the $50,000,000 he had recommended for "defense" was being spent for all-out preparation —ships, recruiting, supplies, etc.—not only for an invasion of Cuba, but also for an attack on the Philippines.

Miss Leech prefers to accept McKinley's prewar statements at their face value: a great President trying his best to keep the country out of war. Villard, as we have seen, was a leader of the minority belief that McKinley was only stalling until he thought the country was properly prepared to take the offensive. Miss Leech makes very little of the Woodford message to McKinley apprising him of the Spanish offer of surrender. She does not even state what the message contained—among other concessions, the guarantee that the Queen Regent had agreed to suspend all hostilities in Cuba

176

for at least six months, thus giving the United States the opportunity of mediating between the rebels and the loyalist Cubans and setting up a democratic form of government. The message was, in fact, nothing less than an invitation to the United States to move into Cuba without firing a shot.

As the book goes on, in the course of some 30 immensely detailed pages about the days leading up to the President's speech to Congress and the resulting declaration of war, it is not even mentioned that McKinley omitted to give the main contents of the message from Spain; nor that at the end of his speech he quoted a couple of the less important paragraphs from the Woodford cable, giving the impression that the message was of no real import to the state of affairs in Cuba. But what is perhaps strangest of all, *In the Days of McKinley,* in its one direct reference to the Woodford cable, mentions briefly that "General Woodford had cabled a prophesy of peace. . . ." No date is given, though the message was received the day before McKinley was to deliver his speech to Congress asking for war.

This is as close as the author ever comes to describing what amounted to a virtually unconditional surrender offer, a document which, had it been made public and properly implemented, might well have prevented a disastrous and costly war involving the lives of millions. Yet here we find it referred to merely as a "prophesy of peace" (whatever that is supposed to mean) with the implication that it could have had no real relevance to the buildup for war.

The situation at the time of the President's speech to Congress is summed up with the sentence: "The President had consummately failed, not in the conduct of his diplomacy, but in restraining the belligerence of Congress and the American people." It remains a mystery to me just how the concealment of the Spanish surrender message was expected to aid in restraining the belligerence of Congress and the people. According to Villard and others, the significant content of the Woodford message was not publicly revealed until three years after the war, when it was discovered by an *Evening Post* reporter. (By which time, as is true after any war, at least until all those who have been involved are long gone, nobody wanted to be reminded of such embarrassing facts.)

I have gone into all this quite deliberately for the purpose of casting reasonable doubt on the credibility of the witness —in this case a book called *In the Days of McKinley*. For it is this book, more than any other, which has preserved and embellished all the old myths of the Miles haters, largely derived from the Pulitzer press of 1888-1901. And such a book, if not challenged, could play quite a part in keeping our poor commanding general of the Army forever well buried in the pages of history under dusty layers of old vilifications.

Miss Leech introduces the General in a long denigrating paragraph. It begins with the comment that the post of commanding general was an "honorary sinecure" and that the incumbent "did not, as his title implied, exercise command." (This amazing statement is, however, completely if tacitly contradicted later in the text, when it becomes necessary to refer to Miles' active direction of the troops in Cuba and Puerto Rico.) The nearest thing to any hint of Miles' having for twenty years been the most successful commander in the Indian campaigns, and his championing of the rights of the Indians, is a contemptuous phrase to the effect that he was once "nicknamed" the Indian Fighter. And the paragraph ends with the accusation that Miles "dreamed of becoming President" and was a "born troublemaker and a tireless promoter of his own interest . . . ," though admitting he was a handsome figure of a man in uniform, his chest covered with medals. (Nothing said about where all those medals came from.) It is interesting to note that no such personal bias is applied to any other of McKinley's generals. William Shafter, for example, the grotesquely obese and undistinguished commander of the expeditionary force in Cuba (*un-*

der Miles), whose appointment was well known to be the result of his political support of McKinley, is described with almost downright affection.

The opening diatribe sets the pace for all subsequent mention of Miles in the book. The waspish tone reserved for him is not even applied to McKinley's assassin. And when Miles is finally dropped from the story altogether, though at a point well before his retirement as commander of the Army, the author, commenting that the General had faded from the political scene, leaves him with the final barb that it was an obscurity "he so richly deserved."

Why should such a talented researcher as Miss Leech, more than thirty years after the venerable old gentleman's death, harbor such venom for him? She does admit, at one point in her text, though with a minimum of detail and no word of praise, that he alone saved the country from a colossal disaster when McKinley prematurely ordered him to embark for Cuba with 70,000 men.

This incident seems to me to be one of the most significant in Miles' entire career. It occurred just 30 days after the President's decision to go to war had been ratified by Congress. The whole military establishment was still in a state of tremendous confusion and disorganization. The sudden expansion of the Army, from 25,000 men to more than 100,-000, had caused almost insurmountable problems of supply and transportation. It had been necessary to disperse nearly all the regular Army officers, from corporals on up, to staff the volunteer outfits, with chaotic results. (Miles wanted to hold the flood of volunteers in check, but the War Department had overridden him.)

At the height of the confusion, on May 5, Miles received a direct order from the President directing him to take personal command of the Eastern forces, numbering 70,000, and to proceed at once to invade Cuba. The General left no record of his reaction to the order, but it may be guessed it did not improve his already despairing opinion of the military judgment of the McKinley regime. In any case, saying nothing to anyone, he left his office as soon as he had read the order, hurried to the White House, and asked to see the President. McKinley did not keep him waiting, and the two conferred for perhaps a couple of hours.

Miles explained that at this initial stage of preparation it would be suicidal to try to send such a force into Cuba. The Spaniards wouldn't even need to put up a fight—there weren't enough provisions on hand to feed the Army for more than a few days. Also ammunition was still in short supply; many Army units had none at all, and there was no prospect of the manufacturers' being able to supply them for at least another month or two. There were railroad snarl-ups all over the country due to the sudden effort to move great numbers of men and trainloads of supplies to the Florida area. The Navy had practically nothing available in the way of transport, and requisitioning of the necessary number of ships for an invasion had barely been started.

This situation was vastly complicated by the fact that the Army Quartermaster Corps and certain other noncombatant departments were not directed by the commander of the Army. (Miles had long deplored this but to no avail.) They were more or less autonomous, taking their orders only from the War Department, which in the McKinley Administration meant from the President himself. Secretary of War Alger was seldom trusted to take the initiative in any important decisions, and was notoriously unqualified to do so. He had been chosen for his talents at carrying out purely political functions—it is safe to say McKinley, when appointing him, had not anticipated war, or at any event a war of such magnitude as had been building up in recent months.

McKinley's order to Miles had been brought on by many pressures on the President—the Congress, the newspapers, and much of the public at large, were all screaming for immediate action. The mysterious sinking of the *Maine*, with the loss of so many of its crew, had widely been accepted, thanks to the yellow press and the warmongers, as a Spanish atrocity that must be avenged. The careful report of the affair, prepared by a commission McKinley had appointed, had not implicated the Spaniards with any concrete evidence, but the report had been of little use against the national tide of war hysteria.

By the end of the conference, McKinley was convinced that Miles' judgment was sound and he rescinded the invasion order. Miles wanted six months to prepare the expeditionary force, while McKinley still hoped the troops could be embarked much sooner. But for the moment, an undertaking that could only have resulted in a military disaster had been averted.

Nothing could have been more fortunate for the country at that uncertain time in its history, on the brink of its first overseas war, than the circumstance that it was Miles who was commanding general of the Army. Of the five other major generals who had been possible choices when Miles was appointed, it is very improbable that any one of them would have had both the judgment and the force of persuasion required to make McKinley change his mind.

Miles was regarded with the greatest respect by most of his colleagues in the regular Army for his insistence on a sound and practical policy of preparation for the troops. But his enemies, among them the prowar newspapers, remembering he had been opposed to the war, accused him of holding back. He was even blamed for all the deficiencies and delays of the supply departments over which he had been given no control.

20

WHAT existed at the start of the war with Spain was a strange alignment, apparently misinterpreted and misunderstood ever since. General Miles, the commander of the Army—more than sixty years afterward still being damned as a military opportunist—was actually on the side of the great liberals of his day. He had strongly stated his position against the war and against imperialistic expansion, making him both mistrusted and hated by Hearst, Pulitzer, Roosevelt, Dewey, certain generals who saw a chance in the Philippines to become heroes, many Congressmen, and others. (McKinley, an astute politician and judge of men, recognized that Miles was still his safest choice to plan and direct the field operations of the war.) Most liberals, however, not recognizing a potentially powerful ally, ignored Miles. As a military man he could not be admitted to their sacrosanct fraternity. Perhaps it would have helped if he had been a Harvard man.

Though Miles' views were given little notice on the national scene, he was still a popular figure in his home state of Massachusetts. When he spoke in Boston, crowds turned out to applaud him. Unfortunately, by that time the great liberal intellectual community of Massachusetts, long dominated by such names as Thoreau, Garrison, Emerson, Eliot, Phillips, and Taussig, was on the wane.

On the national and international scene, Massachusetts was

now represented by Senator Henry Cabot Lodge, who, like most of his Massachusetts Senatorial successors, even to the present, was a master at the political game of always ending up on the winning side. In the case of the Spanish-American War, Lodge foresaw at the outset that it was the younger, tough-talking, empire-promoting Teddy Roosevelt, and not the politically unpopular top commander of the Army, who would most likely emerge as the military hero of the day. And it may be remembered that seventeen years later, while Woodrow Wilson was still trying to prevent the United States involvement in World War I, it was Lodge again who so effectively ridiculed and reviled the Administration's peace efforts.

Perhaps most of us, even in our own vastly more sophisticated times, instinctively try to disown any army commander who openly denounces any kind of a war in which he himself must serve—the idea being that military men should just do their jobs and leave it to enlightened civilians to decide whether or not the war is justifiable. Perhaps Miles had so sealed his fate in history by his attitude *before* the war with Spain that his subsequent brilliant conduct in the war itself would neither be widely recognized nor very long remembered.

Miles also took an unpopular view with regard to the Philippine Islands question. He saw no justification, on military grounds, for attacking Spain in an area halfway around the world, since it could have no bearing on the outcome of the war in the Caribbean. And he denounced the scheme of the expansionists in the government, who planned to use the war in Cuba as an excuse for annexing the Philippines. History finally caught up with the Miles viewpoint half a century later, when in 1946 we finally granted the Philippines the independence we had denied them after defeating the Spanish at Manila in 1898. That denial, incidentally, cost us an ensuing three bloody years of warfare often described later

183

by historians as the most infamous in our history. But these facts, unfortunately, could hardly help to enhance Miles' reputation during his own lifetime.

It was not only from his extensive study of military history that Miles had become so opposed to the policy of territorial expansion by means of armed force. For thirty years, in one Indian campaign after another, he had to deal first-hand with the sad results of government efforts to "pacify" and "civilize" the Indian nations of the West. It is easy enough to see why he had little confidence in any government plans for U.S. intervention abroad.

By the time of the war with Spain, at the peak of the new wave of national enthusiasm for making the nation into an imperialistic power, Miles had become a unique anachronism among the important Army and Navy figures of that period. In action a hardheaded realist, with a lifetime of success as a field commander behind him, he was also a humanitarian with a deep belief in racial equality and the rights of small nations to govern themselves. Miles found little support for some of his beliefs in his own time; even today the Miles views on foreign policy would not be widely approved, and least of all within the military establishment.

But here it might be restated that Miles' niche in American military history should not be determined on the basis of his brand of philosophy. Two points alone should serve to re-establish his importance, once and for all: the historically significant posts he held, and his record of actual accomplishment. If we assess the importance of Hitler's generals solely on the basis of their accomplishments, surely we should do as much for one of our own.

While Miles the realist was working day and night to build up an army equipped for the kind of war anticipated, Miles the idealist was still trying to help avert that war by making his unwanted views known to the Administration and the newspapers. The General himself rather conservatively summarized his prewar position in *Serving the Republic,* published in 1911, eight years after his retirement.

As to the necessity of the war with Spain, it is believed that arbitration could have settled the international controversy. We know from the statement of our own minister at Madrid, General Stewart L. Woodford, that the Spanish ministry and the Queen Regent tried loyally and in good faith to grant and enforce such autonomy as they thought would secure peace and order in Cuba. I had a good opportunity of knowing the disposition of many of the prominent men of our country, especially President McKinley and his Cabinet, and I know that only one of the latter was in favor of war. I know that John Sherman, the Secretary of State, one of the few pre-eminent statesmen of our country, was decidedly opposed to it, and deemed it unnecessary; whereas, on the other hand, I heard a conversation between one member of the Cabinet and an assistant secretary, which was as follows: The assistant secretary said to the member of the Cabinet, "What are you doing toward getting up a war with Spain?" The member of the Cabinet replied, "I am practically alone in the administration, but I am doing all I can to bring it about." The assistant secretary, with great gusto, replied, "Thank God! thank God!"

It is obvious that the "assistant secretary" was Theodore Roosevelt, then assistant to John D. Long, Secretary of the Navy. (Roosevelt, as acting secretary part of the time when Long was ill or on vacation, had been working hard to push the Navy into readiness for an attack on Manila.) And Long was probably the cabinet member Miles claimed was the only one, at the outset of the buildup for war, who favored it. As for Secretary of War Alger, he was taunted by McKinley, some months before the President came out openly for war, for his policy of being prowar and antiwar on alternate weeks.

In his book Miles continued with some observations about the sinking of the *Maine.*

> I have never believed that the disaster was caused by the Spanish government nor its officials or agents. They certainly had no motive for such a crime, and every reason to avoid it. . . . I believe that the disaster resulted from internal rather than external causes.

Unfortunately for his standing with the Administration, Miles had made his opinion public after the official report on the *Maine* affair was released, shortly before war was declared. From mid-February, when the battleship *Maine* had been blown up at Havana—or, as Miles believed, had blown itself up accidentally—until April, while awaiting the final report of his commission of investigation, McKinley held at bay the forces demanding immediate military reprisal. When the report was finally delivered at the White House, the whole country was waiting to learn its conclusions. Even before it was officially released the next morning, someone leaked out the news that the commission had decided the explosion was caused by some external cause such as a mine.

This was all that was needed for the prowar newspapers from coast to coast to run off banner headlines screaming that it had now been proved the *Maine* had been sunk by the Spaniards. The public at large was readily convinced, and thousands more volunteers swamped the already crowded recruiting stations. *The sinking of the Maine must be avenged!*

Actually the report contained nothing to indicate who, if anyone, had placed explosives under the ship. Evidence that the explosion had been caused externally, and not by internal accident, was largely conjectural and not very convincing. From the uncertain findings of Navy divers, groping about in the murky depths, it was decided the shape and position of the breach in the hull indicated an external cause. A Spanish investigating team, from the same evidence, con-

186

cluded the cause must have been internal. But their report was of course not even taken seriously in the United States.

For General Miles, after the government and the public at large had accepted the official U.S. verdict, to calmly repeat that he still believed the disaster had been caused by some internal accident, thus supporting the report of the hated Spaniards, must have taken courage of a sort that seemed downright foolhardy. At any rate, the country was by then in such a furor that no attention was paid to Miles' statement, within the government or elsewhere. The commanding general was given no time to further expound his views, but was kept on the wires between Tampa and Washington in the frantic effort to ship troops and equipment to the Southern embarkation ports. He had been saddled with 100,000 more volunteers than he had recommended, and the resulting confusion was enormous.

Early in May, Miles was informed by the President that it had been decided to destroy the Spanish fleet stationed in the Philippines. He was ordered to prepare a force of 15,000 troops to be sent out to the Pacific to occupy an anticipated base there. Few Americans at the time foresaw the plans of Roosevelt and others to annex the whole territory of the Philippines. Miles himself expected the campaign would lead only to the establishment of a naval base in the islands, such as the one we were to retain after the war in Cuba, at Guantánamo. As he wrote afterward:

I recommended [in the spring of 1898] that troops be sent there under General Anderson, and designated the regiments and batteries, together with high-power guns, mortars, and ammunition, to fortify and hold certain strategic positions in the archipelago, believing our government would always hold strong naval positions in the Orient; but I did not suppose we would ever assume to acquire the territory against the will of the people thereof. . . .

Actually the decision to acquire the Philippines, and indeed the whole new concept of territorial expansion, was very profoundly influenced and supported by an event which most Spanish-American War students have somehow failed to take into account in this respect—the acquisition of the Territory of Hawaii, which also took place in 1898. In the light of later decades of worldwide disillusionment with colonies, protectorates, and colonialism generally, the history of Hawaii seems an unbelievable fairy story. Over the centuries, there had been a few attempts by various European nations to take control, but they had proved short and unsuccessful, and the islands remained independent. In 1851 the reigning king offered to join his country to the United States, but Daniel Webster persuaded Congress to refuse the offer. American traders and missionaries went out anyway in considerable numbers, and many remained to become influential citizens. By 1885 it had become well established that the United States was a sort of unofficial protector, and trade and reciprocity treaties were enacted. A revolution in 1893 (not much bloodshed) resulted in the U.S.-fostered Republic of Hawaii. Its first, and last, president, Sanford B. Dole, spent most of his unselfish career in office working to ally his country with the States. This was quietly accomplished, and in the summer of 1898 Hawaii was annexed and, two years later, became a U.S. territory.

The only price we paid for this rich, remote paradise, with its all-important naval and military potential in the area of the Pacific, was the assumption of a $4,000,000 national debt! (In contrast, after seizing the Philippines, we decided to pay Spain $30,000,000—which in retrospect would seem to have been a gesture to convince the world we hadn't really stolen the islands, we had merely purchased them. But we were to find that the Filipinos would take a somewhat different view.)

And so it was the view of the expansionists that since we

had now acquired Hawaii so easily, why not keep right on across the Pacific, with the Philippines next. Incredible as it may now seem, in 1898 most Americans, from the President on down, hadn't the haziest notion of the vast differences between Hawaii and the Philippines. (On second thought, perhaps it doesn't seem so incredible, considering how little we still know about Vietnam even after having landed a large army there.)

Hawaii had already become Americanized to a great extent. A dozen or so missionary families had stayed on for generations and become large landowners. The naval base and trading companies had brought in many more Americans. English had long been the national language. Health standards were among the highest in the world, and education was no problem.

The area of the Philippines (114,400 square miles) was about nineteen times greater than that of Hawaii. Population was probably 10 to 12 million; that of Hawaii was about 300,000. Practically no English was spoken in the Philippines. Though under Spanish rule for more than three centuries, only an elite minority spoke Spanish. Various tribal groups, numbering into the millions, had never been either "civilized" or to any extent subjugated. On some of the islands the most savage forms of intertribal warfare had been an established way of life since prehistory.

The educated minority considered themselves to be as much a part of the "white" race as their compatriots in Spain, and their oldest university had been founded before 1600. (Yet it is a fact that during our first years of so-called occupation, our military and civil dignitaries refused to entertain socially any natives, however educated or distinguished, on the grounds that Filipinos were "colored.") For more than a century the educated Filipinos had been building up an impassioned nationalism, a movement which had all the force of a religious fanaticism.

But the import of all this we would only learn, disastrously and expensively, through the experiences of the next forty years of Philippine occupation. In 1898 the thinking in Washington was that if we were to send out a few people to educate the lower classes, teach them English, and set up a "democratic" form of territorial government, they would soon be as happy and grateful as the Hawaiians. Apparently nobody in our government had any idea that a great many Filipinos might be willing to fight just as desperately and interminably against American rule as they had fought against Spanish rule.

Again it may be said that Miles stood stubbornly alone, among our military commanders, in his skeptical view of the Philippine situation. But at the time, he was confined by the President to preparing for operations in Cuba and Puerto Rico. He would have to wait until some time after the war with Spain had been concluded before he could get to the Philippines himself to survey the military scene there. Then he would try to assess the irreparable damage already done by our army of occupation to Philippine-American relations.

21

ONE of the better accounts of the causes of the war and events leading up to it is found in *The Martial Spirit,* by Walter Millis. In this book, as in so many others about the Spanish-American conflict, only the briefest possible mention is made of the commanding general of the Army—the man who held the highest military post in the war the book sets out to describe in such complete detail. There are only a few items in all, and none which had not been written a hundred times before in almost the same words. In the first hundred-plus pages, concerning the months preceding the war, there is only one short line about Miles. He is named as the commander of the Army at the time and identified only as the general who had commanded the final Indian campaigns. It is *not* mentioned that he had been commanding the Army since 1895; and there is not a word about his age, appearance, background, character, experience, or military record.

There is, however, in the book's further occasional short references to Miles, a distinct trace of the approach so virulently exaggerated by Miss Leech in her later work. For example, Millis states that a few weeks before the start of the war, it "occurred to General Miles" that the Army was in no shape for an invasion of Cuba, and some drastic action should be taken at once in the way of preparation and equipment. One almost gets the impression Miles had just awakened from a kind of Rip Van Winkle sleep when it "occurred" to him something should be done about the condition of the Army.

Of course, as I have indicated, Miles had been working desperately, and quite vocally, for three or four years trying to induce Congress and the Administration to enlarge the Army and to improve and expand its equipment, from long-range field pieces to modern machine guns and infantry rifles. It *could* have been said, with some truth, that only when war was imminent had it "occurred" to McKinley and his congressional leaders that they had better begin to act on Miles' often repeated entreaties.

Such a ridiculously false impression of Miles' position with regard to the expansion and preparation of the Army, it seems to me, could have come from but one source—the newspapers of the period, notably, the prowar yellow journals. Naturally most of the journalists, who despised Miles for his "unpatriotic" antiwar opinions, blamed him savagely as commander of the Army for its every shortcoming. What is perhaps more pertinent to our search for the *real* Miles is that whenever they were *not* blaming him for something, they deliberately and persistently ignored him. The fact that Miles with equal persistence ignored the journalists, for whom he had no more liking than they had for him, only serves to strengthen the point. Thus the vital constructive part being played by Miles in preparing the Army for the Spanish-American War was little mentioned in the press of those days, and consequently little mentioned by historians afterward.

Nevertheless, as old War Department records show, it was Miles, and Miles alone, who had long been preparing detailed plans and studies for expanding the Army and modernizing its equipment and training. Had no such plans been available, the rapid preparation that preceded the war would have been long delayed at best.

When war was declared, Miles foresaw great difficulty with

the departments of equipment and supply. He requested that his authority be extended, or his rank raised to lieutenant general, so that the Quartermaster Corps would come under his command. The Secretary of War refused. Alger wanted to keep control of this potentially profitable arm of the military himself, and he proceeded to load it with his friends and political appointees. As a result certain necessary equipment and supplies would be ordered for shipment to Florida, and the Army unit supposed to receive the shipment would not even be notified. Before long officers were grabbing whatever supplies they could find, without regard to where the stuff had been assigned.

Meanwhile thousands more troops, both regular and volunteer regiments, were pouring into Tampa, the main embarkation point. Miles thought he had sent enough able commanders there to handle the situation, having been ordered himself to remain at his Washington headquarters. But in a few weeks it was reported that the almost total disorganization at Tampa was verging on disaster. Some regiments had been without food for days, others had no quarters assigned. Alger's sending down many more thousands of volunteers than had been provided for, under newly appointed and inexperienced general officers, had disrupted the whole operation.

When the War Department and the President finally began to realize the gravity of the Tampa mix-up, they decided to give their commanding general a little more freedom of movement and generously allowed him to go down himself. Perhaps he could straighten things out down there—certainly nobody else had been able to.

When Miles got off the train at Tampa, in the first intense heat of the summer, some of the troops were already starting to board the transports. Thirty-two ships had been assembled, with an escort of sixteen Navy vessels. There was no plan assigning the various units to the transports. Or if there was one, nobody was paying any attention to it. Cavalry, infantry, and artillery units fought among each other for space on this ship or that, without regard to its stated capacity. Some regiments were hopelessly split up into wandering, lost groups, unable to find their commanders.

Lt. Col. Theodore Roosevelt was there with the volunteer Rough Riders regiment he had raised (without benefit of any previous military training) and was acting so much like its commander that several newspaper men referred to him as such, throughout the war. The actual commander was Col. Leonard Wood, a seasoned protégé of Miles and the Army surgeon who later became one of the famous generals of World War I. Recently granted leave from his post as Assistant Secretary of the Navy, the popular "Teddy" did his bit during the embarkation confusion by rushing down to the best ship, the *Yucatan,* and climbing aboard with his Rough Riders. The General plunged into this melee at the port, thundering orders right and left, with the desperate energy of a tough field commander rushing up to rally his front lines in a hot battle.

The Secretary of War had sent a direct order to Shafter that he was to embark his whole expeditionary force and leave for Cuba immediately. Miles had only a few hours to try to make some kind of improvement in the chaotic disposition of the troops and remedy some of the worst situations regarding missing equipment and supplies. There was no use now in wiring Alger that the troops were not yet ready. Shafter had assured Alger that he was prepared to embark, and the Secretary of War still had complete faith in the bumbling 350-pound commander of the expeditionary force. Shafter had already been hoisted aboard one of the ships, and was serenely waiting for the convoy to set sail.

Before the last vessels of this hopelessly disorganized and haphazardly equipped flotilla had left the port, those already standing out to sea were signaled to return. Spanish warships were thought to have been sighted in the Caribbean, according to a Navy report that reached Washington, and the Secretary of War had developed a sudden panic. In a few days it was decided the report must have been a false alarm, and again orders came for the convoy to set out at once for Cuba. But those few days may have made the difference between certain disaster and a reasonable chance for the success of the expedition. Missing supplies were located and loaded, various mixed-up units were sorted out and rearranged, and the whole plan of operation was somewhat less chaotic on the second departure. But for thousands of troops suffering from short rations and little water, it meant several more days of agony in the terribly crowded, sweltering quarters belowdecks. To the furious dismay of General Miles, about half the regiments were being sent off on this tropical campaign, in summer heat, unsupplied with any other uniforms than the heavy winter woolens they were wearing.

For whatever reasons, American history has a way of regarding certain wars of the past as "popular" and others as "unpopular" forever afterward. And furthermore, how we may come to regard a war after it is over seems to have nothing to do with how we may have regarded it at the time. When the troops embarked for Cuba, the general enthusiasm for war had reached a peak—much more nearly a unanimity of opinion than the country has ever since shown, in fact, on the question of armed intervention. Yet the set of factors which led to that nearly universal approval and enthusiasm in 1898 sound almost identical to those factors which today we are told, by all proponents of the Vietnam War, have led us into that present conflict.

In both cases there were three main objectives. First, to halt the political domination of a small country by a larger power we regarded as hostile to our own interests or way of life. Second, to aid one local armed faction—be it called the Rebels or the Patriots or the Nationalists or whatever—to destroy another local faction, or factions, in order to set up a "democratic" form of government. Third (though less publicized, it is taken for granted), to retain more or less permanent military bases on the scene of action after it is over. But a distinguishing and most remarkable aspect of the Spanish-American War, as it turned out, was its short duration—only a little more than three months, with most of the action taking place in a few weeks.

Nobody had even time to write a book about it, either for or against, until it was already past history. When, finally, accurate and objective books were written, the war had generally come to be regarded as one of the "unpopular" variety. It has followed that in the past quarter-century or more, no publisher in his right mind would think of putting out a book about the Spanish-American War that did not represent that conflict as somewhat ridiculous, ill advised, unnecessary, scandalously conducted, etc., etc. This is made clear by the titles alone. In a popular recent work, *The Splendid Little War*, the author, Frank Freidel, cites two outstanding earlier books, Gregory Mason's *Remember the Main* and Walter Millis' *The Martial Spirit*, and refers to these books as being "satiric"—and so, of course, is his own.

For purposes of comparison, the War of 1812—to choose one example—came to be regarded historically as a "popular" war. But when it began, very many Americans, the majority perhaps, opposed it. And it is interesting to review the relative importance we have accorded, historically, to the military leaders in each of these two wars. Best known in the Spanish-American War were Miles, Shafter, Wheeler, Wood, Anderson, Chaffee, Funston, Goethals, Lawton, W. S. Lee, Wilson, A. MacArthur. In contrast to these soon more or less forgotten heroes, we have only to think of 1812 and such legendary names come to mind as Andrew Jackson, Sam Houston, Davy Crockett, and William H. Harrison.

Concluding this line of thought, our main concern is to find the real factors which caused Miles to be more featured in the news, and be more of a national hero, in the years preceding the war with Spain than he was afterward. And this in spite of his own personal record of success in that war, a record unassailable by even his most biased critics. Paradoxical though it may sound, it is reasonable to assume that had Miles been retired just before the war instead of just after, he might have been much better remembered by historians ever since—perhaps even as one of the most eminent commanding generals of the Army, in terms of overall service and accomplishments, of the nineteenth century. In any case, the fact remains that he has *not* been so remembered, but has been largely neglected by some historians and briefly lampooned by others whenever they dealt with that period of his career which began *after* the romantic Indian-fighting years.

By the time war was actively started, with the expeditionary force on its way to Cuba, Miles had already been maneuvered out of the spotlight usually accorded commanding generals of the Army during wartime. McKinley and Alger, having decided to send their own man, Shafter, to Cuba, intended to keep Miles in Washington where he could be found if needed, but confined to routine duties hardly noticed by a national press avid for more sensational news. It was obvious that Miles was not going to be forgiven, by the Administration, by the press, or by anyone else, for having once stated that he thought the war was unnecessary and unjustified, or for having opposed the useless, hysterical, and hasty induction of 300,000 volunteers—an action which had nearly wrecked the operating efficiency of the whole military establishment at the outset of the war.

22

GENERAL Shafter began his landing operations at Daiquiri on June 22. And for the next three weeks, about
the duration of the campaign, events more than justified the
"satiric" descriptions of later historians. Though it may be that
not very much humor in the situation was seen by several thousand troops laid low by malaria, food poisoning, dysentery,
yellow fever, and—a few of them—by Spanish bullets. (Miles
had tried in vain to persuade the War Department to wait for
sufficient supplies of the modern smokeless powder; Spanish
sharpshooters could easily spot any frontline American who
fired a gun, just by the cloud of black smoke that revealed his
exact position.)

The lumbering, bumbling Shafter had conceived a plan
worthy of the best military thinking of the early Middle Ages.
From Daiquiri and Siboney, a few miles east of Santiago
harbor where the Spanish fleet was anchored, he planned to
march his forces through roadless swamps and jungles to Santiago, and lay siege to that well-defended and nearly impreg-
nable military citadel. Every movement was advertised to the
waiting enemy.

It has never been figured out why the Spanish commander
didn't send out a few thousand troops to greet Shafter's
totally disorganized and almost defenseless landing operations. The Spanish could have easily slaughtered a large num-

ber of the troops landing on the open beaches. But it may be that Toral foresaw ultimate defeat and deliberately decided to fight only defensively.

In any case, as the Americans marched toward Santiago the Spanish fought only a series of delaying skirmishes, among them the famed San Juan Hill affair. In Roosevelt's book about the Rough Riders, San Juan is described in such heroic rhetoric it appears to have been the decisive battle of the century, with Teddy himself in the role of the fearless leader who rallied his men against insuperable odds and saved the day. Actually, besides the Rough Riders regiment, at least six thousand other troops were engaged, under two general officers; and in all, something like a hundred Americans were killed at San Juan. This was, however, the highest number killed in a single battle except at El Caney, the same day, where losses were similar; relatively high figures, considering that only 369 American soldiers were killed in action throughout the entire war.

In the meantime, several thousand Cuban rebel troops had cut off the rail supply lines to Santiago and were making a few haphazard attacks on various outposts. But they were very scantily supplied, and Shafter had accomplished little or no effective liaison with them.

General Miles was preparing a second expeditionary force for the invasion of Puerto Rico, trying to obtain permission to lead it himself. It was the safest way, he was confident, of avoiding any repetition of the many hideous blunders already well known to have occurred in Cuba. These blunders had been thoroughly publicized by a hundred or so war correspondents on the scene, many of whom had managed to get around any form of censorship.

There was in Cuba almost no organized transport between the front lines and the beachhead some fifteen miles distant. The ill and wounded who could still walk had to make it on foot. Often the men had no food for two or three days at a time. Medical supplies were woefully inadequate, and hospital facilities almost nonexistent. Sanitary conditions in the camps were said to be totally out of control; malaria was general, and yellow fever was starting to spread, with more than a hundred cases already reported. Communications were so lacking that most field commanders were operating largely on their own judgment and initiative.

Miles was still in the States on July 3, when Admiral Pascual Cervera's Spanish fleet tried to escape from Santiago and was totally destroyed by the U.S. fleet lying in wait just outside the harbor. Because Nelson A. Miles, long afterward, was to become curiously involved in the aftermath of that battle—an affair which would have a lasting effect on his reputation—a few details of the historic naval engagement may be in order.

The U.S. Atlantic squadron, consisting of eight heavy warships and assorted other craft, for several weeks had been guarding the entrance to Santiago harbor; inside lay the Spanish fleet of four heavy ships and two destroyers. It was not known by the Americans that the Spanish ships were antiquated, slow, and vastly inferior in armament and fire power compared to the U.S. ships.

The U.S. fleet was commanded by acting Rear Admiral William T. Sampson, a career Navy officer with an apparently very creditable service record dating back to the start of the Civil War. Second in command was Commodore Winfield S. Schley, of similar background. Beneath an imposing appearance, Sampson was a vain and self-centered man who managed to combine a supreme arrogance with constant timidity.

During the whole month Sampson's ships had been keeping the Spanish fleet bottled up in Santiago harbor, his only plan of battle consisted of posting his ships in a wide line to enable an immediate attack on the Spaniards if they should try to escape out to sea. Though he had unlimited coal at a nearby base set up at Guantánamo, several of his captains had been ordered to stand by with most of their boilers shut down, presumably to save fuel. He was also in great fear of approaching anywhere near the shore batteries, apparently unaware that the Spanish had only such ancient cannon there that it would have been a miracle if one of his ships were hit even at close range.

On the early dawn of July 3, Sampson decided to confer with Shafter, who for days had been sending urgent messages trying to get him to bring his ships closer in and launch a naval bombardment of Santiago in support of an Army assault. Despite the fact that one of his largest ships, the *Massachusetts*, was already absent that morning to take on coal at Guantánamo, Sampson took a second one, the *New York*, his own flagship, together with two smaller escort ships, away from their stations in the fleet lineup, to transport him to Siboney, where he planned to go ashore and ride seven miles inland to the headquarters of the ailing Shafter. So when Cervera's ships suddenly dashed out of the harbor and tried to make a run for it up the west coast, Sampson was just landing at Siboney, and the U.S. fleet was lacking two of its best ships. As Miles was to remark long afterward, had those two ships been needed to avert any sort of disaster, Sampson would surely have been responsible for their absence.

Fortunately the remaining ships of the fleet, under Commodore Schley—four battleships, one cruiser and two armed yachts—were overwhelmingly superior to the Spanish ships. The latter were foul-bottomed and in very poor repair, and while able to make their escape out of the harbor because of the time it took for some of the U.S. ships to get up steam, they were quickly overtaken. Their fire power was deplorable, and they were never able to register a direct hit on any U.S. ship.

One by one, the Spanish ships were sunk along the beach by Schley's pursuing squadron. It might be added that the U.S. ships' guns were not miraculously accurate either—122 hits out of 9,433 shots fired. Hundreds were killed and wounded among the Spanish crews. The Americans lost only one seaman, whose head was taken off by a cannonball passing over the top deck of a battleship.

When Sampson heard the shooting begin, he at once started full-speed back up the coast aboard the *New York*. But because the battle was moving along ahead of him, by the time he could finally catch up, later in the day, the shooting was all over. Schley signaled the approaching *New York,* apprising Sampson of the great and complete victory. To which Sampson signaled back three words: "Report your casualties." Disgusted and hurt beyond expression at this terse lack of courtesy or congratulation on the part of his superior, Schley replied: "One dead, two wounded."

Schley sent a detailed account of the battle ashore to be wired to Washington. This was anticipated and intercepted by the crafty Sampson, who sent instead a message of his own, beginning, "The fleet under my command offers the nation, as a Fourth of July present, the whole of Cervera's fleet." This amazing dispatch hardly conveyed the impression that Sampson and his flagship had nothing whatever to do with the great battle except to help rescue some of the survivors. And there was no mention whatever of Commodore Schley. So much, for the moment, concerning the Sampson-Schley affair. It was not to involve Miles until some three years later.

Commodore George Dewey had already destroyed the Spanish fleet in Manila Bay on May 1, in a much more expeditious and efficiently planned manner than that of the belated Santiago action. Now with both Spanish fleets gone, the only possible outcome of the war was assured. It only remained for the Army to take care of whatever resistance the remaining garrison troops might still offer in the three theaters of the war: Cuba, Puerto Rico, and the Philippines. Spain, of course, after the loss of most of her navy, was in no position to either reinforce or supply the forces on those distant outposts of a long-lost empire.

Consequently, the popular American heroes during the war were the naval commanders. Dewey received unlimited national acclaim and publicity, with Sampson next in line. Meanwhile their opposite numbers in the Army were given relatively little attention. When the commanding general of the Army was mentioned at all, it was usually without reference to the fact that he occupied the top military post. Presumably, to the reading public at large he was just one of several high-ranking generals associated with the Cuba-Puerto Rico area, an impression widely accepted ever since.

It might also be mentioned here again that the commanding general of the Army, at that time, was being given no chance to plan or direct overall operations in such widely separated areas as the Caribbean and the Pacific. In regard to the Philippines, Miles had only been ordered to prepare the expeditionary force and recommend officers to command it. From then on, so far as operations in the Pacific could be directed from Washington, the President and the Secretary of War ran the show, without benefit of advice or interference from their commanding general of the Army.

Miles had reasons for remaining in Washington, other than McKinley's decision to send his own protégé, Shafter, to Cuba in command of the forces there. There was the urgent and complicated business of trying to supply the Cuban rebel forces with arms and ammunition. These had to be procured wherever they could be found, some from foreign countries, and without regard for varying degrees of obsolescence. Half enough modern matériel to equip U.S. troops had still not been produced, and there had not been time enough to manufacture a reserve of ammunition to sustain the war should it last more than a few months. Miles himself had become the chief victim of the situation he tried for so many

203

years to avert by getting Congress to raise more funds for the Army.

The General was also tremendously harassed by the problems of provisioning and finding barracks for the horde of recruits the War Department had accepted. Miles had correctly foreseen that some 200,000 of them would never be needed to perform any useful duty whatever in this war, but once they were in the Army it was his duty to see that they were maintained and organized as efficiently as possible. He was also trying his best to implement the ill-conceived logistics of the Caribbean campaigns, though his own eminently sound plan for taking Puerto Rico first, and then using that island as a base for invading Cuba, had been reversed by the War Department.

When Shafter sent a wire to Washington, after the Spanish fleet had been eliminated and nearly all its surviving crewmen captured, that he would still be unable to take Santiago with his present forces and needed 15,000 more troops, McKinley began to have some doubts about his chosen field commander. The President may have been further disturbed because Shafter, whose greatest virtue was his blunt honesty, reported that he had been confined to his tent for four days during the most critical period of the advance in Santiago. In the savage tropical heat, poor Shafter's gargantuan bulk had nearly done him in; among other ailments, his sagging belly had become so badly chafed by its supporting harness he couldn't mount a horse or even climb into a wagon.

McKinley called Miles to the White House and told him to leave at once for Cuba, taking the troops he had prepared for the invasion of Puerto Rico. The orders were not specific. Shafter was to remain in immediate command of his original forces, but the implication was that Miles was authorized to direct the overall operations to whatever extent might be necessary in order to secure the quickest possible victory.

23

MILES landed in Cuba on July 11 with an additional force of 1,500 troops. Shafter was greatly relieved at his arrival but must also have felt somewhat humiliated. Miles was in the pink of health and, with his usual energy, lost no time in mounting the fastest horse he could find and dashing off to the front lines. As in the old Indian fighting days, his first move was to inspect all troop positions himself. After that, orders would be sure to start flying thick and fast in all directions.

It took Miles less than twenty-four hours to develop detailed and seemingly infallible plans for taking Santiago. Naval commanders were given instructions for a supporting bombardment (Sampson knew better than to try to equivocate with Miles as he had with Shafter), and the rebel forces were given specific orders for their deployment and action.

It was perhaps a greater opportunity for Miles the "glory hunter" than any he had encountered in his whole past career. Here was his chance to demonstrate the skill acquired from a lifelong study of military tactics. The credit for a spectacular victory now would be sure to reflect largely on the senior officer simply because he was there in person rather than behind his desk in Washington. Miles' every move would be broadcast to the world by Richard Harding Davis, Stephen Crane, Frederic Remington, and the rest. All he had to lose was perhaps a few hundred more American soldiers.

When everything was ready, instead of the expected orders, Miles sent word through Shafter's staff to the Spanish commander, General José Toral, requesting an armistice and an interview under a flag of truce. (One is reminded how often Miles averted some bloody battle with the Indians by persuading the ranking chief to come out and parley with him.) In due course Toral appeared with his escort of aides in dress uniform, in the best tradition of Spanish formality. Miles met him with as much pomp and circumstance as Shafter's somewhat sloppy encampment could afford.

Miles began by saying that he had but recently arrived in Cuba, having been sent by his government to conclude the action there at once and at whatever cost. He went on to explain that he had brought a large force of supporting troops ready to take the field. And that, if necessary, up to 50,000 more could be brought by fast steamers. The situation of the Spanish forces at Santiago was therefore hopeless, and he urged that General Toral, in their common interests of preventing any futile loss of human lives, consider his terms of surrender. Those terms included that all Spanish personnel on the island would be granted full amnesty and protection from the rebel forces and returned to Spain, the U.S. government to supply such aid and transportation as might be needed.

Toral requested, and was granted, a stay of time until noon of the next day to decide. And at the appointed time the Spanish general returned and announced that his superior in Havana, Governor General Ramón Blanco, had been authorized by Madrid to surrender on the terms offered. The war in Cuba was over.

Miles at once sent the following wire:

Headquarters Cavalry Division
Before Santiago de Cuba,
July 14, 1898, 12:55 P.M.

THE SECRETARY OF WAR
Washington, D.C.

General Toral formally surrendered the troops of his army corps and division of Santiago on the terms and understanding that his troops would be returned to Spain. General Shafter will appoint commissioners to draw up conditions of arrangements for carrying out the terms of the surrender. This is very gratifying, and General Shafter and the officers and men of his command are entitled to great credit for their tenacity, fortitude, and in overcoming almost insurmountable obstacles they have encountered. A portion of the army has been infected with yellow fever, and efforts will be made to separate those who are infected and those who are free from it, and to keep those which are still on board ship separated from those on shore. Arrangements will be made immediately for carrying out the further instructions of the President and yourself.

Miles,
Major-General, Commanding the Army

Thinking again of those who have accused Miles of seeking the limelight—taking their cue from Theodore Roosevelt and others who were jealously biased—it is revealing to compare the tone of the above dispatch, with its generous references to Shafter, to the dispatch sent by Sampson after the naval battle of Santiago. The "further instructions" doubtless referred to the proposed expedition to take Puerto Rico, which was still under Spanish rule and defended by several thousand Spanish regulars. Miles was expected to remain in command of this expedition himself. McKinley and Alger had been through some very uncertain weeks during the Cuban campaign, while their obese and ailing field commander had fumbled around at Siboney. The fact that Shafter had often been out of touch with his various disorganized forces at the front was embarrassingly revealed by many correspondents on the scene.

The President might still fear Miles' political ambitions and his well-known habit of trying to run the Army in his own autocratic fashion, interpreting War Department orders pretty much as he saw fit whenever he disagreed with them, but McKinley had come to fear even more any repetition of the blundering in the Cuban campaign. The surest way to insure against this seemed to be to give Miles a free hand in Puerto Rico, as Miles himself had earlier tried to explain to the President. McKinley had also learned, before very long, that Secretary Alger's adroitness in politics did not exactly qualify him to plan or to carry out complex military operations.

Miles still had much to do before leaving Cuba, at which time the forces remaining there would once again be under the sole command of Shafter. The human enemy had been conquered, but the yellow fever epidemic was spreading to the point that imminent disaster threatened the troops. The General had some knowledge of the problem; besides the experiences of his years in the southwest and in Mexico, he had taken pains to study whatever recent data he could find on the subject before going to Cuba. He set up inspection teams, organized sanitary corps, and began an immediate segregation of infected troops. Encampments in bad mosquito areas were moved to high ground, and infected facilities were burned to avoid recontamination.

It was later claimed by some, and has of course been repeated over the years, that burning some of the camps resulted only in further hardships for the men. If so, at least the aggressive attempts to improve conditions had a vastly uplifting effect on the morale of the troops. And no sensible historian could seriously question the effectiveness of Miles' program to clean up widespread conditions of water and food contamination.

In accomplishing all this, Miles issued a series of orders to the forces commanded by Shafter; but he did so through Shafter's headquarters, in order to maintain the proper chain-of-command routine. (His own headquarters remained on the transport *Yale,* anchored at Playa del Este.) And in the course of these communications, an exchange ensued between Miles and Shafter that points up a certain comic-opera aspect of the situation.

Miles had asked Shafter to make various movements of encampments, etc., preparatory to embarking such noninfected troops as would be needed in Puerto Rico. He also requested information about the condition and availability of certain of these troop units. He received the following reply:

Siboney, July 17, 1898, 8:48 P.M.

GENERAL MILES,
    On Board *Yale:*
    Letters and orders in reference to movement of camp received and will be carried out. None is more anxious than myself to get away from here. It seems, from your orders given me, that you regard my force as a part of your command. Nothing would give me greater pleasure than serving under you, General, and I shall comply with all your requests and directions, but I was told by the Secretary that you were not to supersede me in command here. I will furnish the information called for as to the condition of the command to Gilmore, Adjutant General, Army Headquarters.

SHAFTER, *Major-General.*

It should be explained that a day or so before Toral's surrender on July 14, Miles had received an order from Secretary of War Alger. This authorized Miles to supervise and direct the terms, and carrying out, of a surrender if it could be obtained; or if not, to proceed with the assault of Santiago as he saw fit. The order could hardly have been interpreted to mean anything other than that Miles was expected to exercise overall command in any circumstances that might arise. Not that the General was at all likely to act any differently, had he received no such order. In any case his answer to Shafter was typical:

Headquarters of the Army
Playa del Este, July 18.

GENERAL SHAFTER:

Telegram received. Have no desire and have carefully avoided any appearance of superseding you. Your command is part of the United States Army, which I have the honor to command, having been duly assigned thereto, and directed by the President to go wherever I thought my presence required and give such general directions as I thought best concerning military matters, and especially directed to go to Santiago for a specific purpose. You will also notice that the order of the Secretary of War of July 13 left the matter to my discretion. I should regret that any event would cause either yourself or any part of your command to cease to be a part of mine.

Very truly yours,
NELSON A. MILES,
Major-General, Commanding the United States Army

Once the implications of this message had been digested by Shafter, he apparently decided never again to tangle with Miles on the subject of being superseded. Miles restored Shafter to a happier state of mind, and retained his good will forever after, by according him full credit for the victory at Santiago and allowing him the honor of accepting the formal surrender of the Spanish generals.

Puerto Rico was known to be defended by about 8,000 Spanish regular troops and 9,000 volunteers, but this caused Miles no great concern. He arranged for naval support (the Spanish now had none available), and did not plan a direct attack on any of the heavily fortified positions. In such attacks he would be badly outnumbered and sure to take heavy losses, as had occurred when Shafter's men were approaching Santiago. The main points of Miles' strategy included landing the troops wherever they would be least expected; dispersing forces into the interior, with carefully planned liaison between the friendly natives and the troops; and finally isolating and surrounding the various Spanish strongholds. In short, Miles hoped to infiltrate more or less the entire island before engaging any concentration of Spanish troops, knowing that the latter would tend to withdraw into their best fortified positions. And if they could be contained in those positions until their supplies ran low, they might surrender without a fight.

From his recent experience in Cuba, Miles had deduced that the Spanish commanders were little interested in trying to put up a determined resistance, but that they were certainly capable of savage, deadly fighting whenever either their concepts of military honor or their reputations back home at Madrid might be threatened. Therefore Miles issued strict orders to all his field officers to the effect that any Spanish units encountered were to be pursued at a distance and with the least possible shooting, so long as they seemed to be retreating toward their main bases.

It was not a plan calculated to bring great glory and renown for valorous action to the commanding general. Miles was immediately criticized by some of the correspondents and military observers for risking disaster to his troops by deploying them throughout the interior where they could be ambushed. It was also said that Miles was foolishly giving the scattered Spanish troops plenty of time to consolidate and prepare for the most effective resistance.

But Miles' preliminary intelligence work had been thorough. His forces were landed at three points along some sixty miles of coast, at Guanica, Ponce, and Arroyo, a section known to have good interconnecting roads along which the different divisions could be moved rapidly, and if necessary

211

brought together for mutual support. At each of the three landing operations, there was hardly even token resistance; just a few wild shots from small groups of hastily retreating Spanish regulars.

This was a far cry from the unhappy confusion of the landing of Shafter's disorganized forces in Cuba. Miles correctly guessed that the lighters he had requested from the Navy might not be forthcoming; he simply made sure himself that at each landing point selected there were plenty of lighters which could easily be commandeered and put to use. A correspondent at Guanica reported that Miles personally went along with the engineers in a small launch to tow out the lighters, and was seen to be vigorously lending a hand with the ropes. Probably he was shouting orders at the same time which could be heard all the way to the center of Guanica.

Miles took about a week to thoroughly organize all his forces ashore before moving them. Communications were set up between the principal commands—under generals Brooke, Wilson, Henry, Haines, and Schwan—and all the officers commanding the various units were given explicit orders regarding the routes they were to take. One by one, all the principal towns would be occupied, and eventually nearly the whole island crisscrossed by troop movements. Meanwhile it was hoped that the Spanish regulars would all be gradually pushed into their main citadel at San Juan.

24

ALL this delayed action was a terrible disappointment to most of the war correspondents. In Cuba they had been able to file daily reports larded with tales of fantastic heroism: last words of dying men crawling through swamps and jungles, terrible conditions in fever-infected camps, and all the rest of it. Here in Puerto Rico hardly a shot was being fired from one day to the next, almost nobody was being killed, and the native population was entertaining the American troops as though they were groups of tourists from a cruise ship.

One well-known correspondent, Stephen Crane, who had written some of the most lurid copy about the Cuban campaign, got tired of waiting for something to happen. He set off by himself along a road leading inland and, on finally reaching a town, took possession of the place, single-handed, in the name of the United States. It wasn't too difficult, as the friendly natives couldn't understand any English and there were no Spaniards within fifty miles.

However disappointed the newsmen and their millions of readers may have been, Miles' meticulous plans worked out so successfully that only a few Americans were wounded in the entire campaign, and only three were killed. The Spanish lost a dozen or so men, and had a somewhat higher percentage of wounded. On August 13, just three weeks after the landings, the Americans were well on the way to having all the Spanish forces rounded up at San Juan and were in control of most of the rest of the country. And at that point, the Madrid government cabled that an armistice was signed, and all fighting was ended.

Certain American newspaper writers, and others not favorable to Miles, took the view that the Puerto Rico campaign had presented no problems worth mentioning. On the other hand, Richard Harding Davis wrote that it was only because of Miles' expert handling of the expedition, his careful planning and skilled use of intelligence agents, that the Spanish forces—potentially capable of putting up as stiff a fight as their Cuban counterparts—had offered so little resistance. But Miles' nonmilitary accomplishments in Puerto Rico have turned out to be of far greater historical import than the purely military action. To appreciate this, we might take a quick look at the status of the three theaters of the war a half century later.

As for the Philippines, the United States finally granted them the independence the Filipino leaders thought we were going to insure in 1898, and which they continued to fight for afterward with endless determination. Our involvement in the Philippines proved costly, bloody, and in the end unsuccessful. Cuba had been given political independence in 1898 but remained to a large extent economically dependent on the United States. The result was a prolonged exploitation, including our domination of her sugar and other industries. This contributed to a succession of unstable, undemocratic, and not very efficient governments, ending up with another situation very much like that of 1898. Only this time it was Soviet Russia which moved in and "freed" the Cubans from United States domination and influence. So we find that the campaign we fought there has resulted, in the long run, in a Cuba that is far more hostile and dangerous to us than she was under Spanish rule.

Puerto Rico in 1898 could hardly have been more similar

214

to Cuba in general character and background. Yet in a recent plebiscite, the people voted almost unanimously in favor of remaining a part of the United States (either as a territory or a state) and *against* independence. Can it be said that the chain of events leading to the Puerto Rico of today was put in motion by one man alone—Nelson A. Miles? At least those Puerto Ricans who are most aware of their own history will answer yes. Though it must be admitted that the cloud of obscurity that settled over Miles has extended, over the years, into Puerto Rico itself to some extent.

When Miles was allowed to command the invasion of Puerto Rico, the War Department, backed by the Administration, expected him to make a direct attack on San Juan, more or less as Shafter's forces had attacked Santiago in Cuba. The U.S. naval commanders, confident and aggressive after their easy victory in Cuba, were eager to begin a bombardment of the fortified city as a prelude to a mass landing of the Army.

But Miles informed the fleet commanders that as he was directing the invasion, the role of the Navy was to perform only where and when he should specify, supporting him as he might decide best. (Privately he felt that certain admirals had already claimed far more credit for the success of the war than they deserved.) Unlike Shafter, who had been unable to achieve any cooperation from Admiral Sampson and the fleet, Miles was either feared or respected to the extent that the naval commanders did not dare to refuse his orders. So there was no shelling of San Juan by the fleet, and Miles landed at the other end of the island. Only a few shots were called for, aimed at Spanish outposts, to cover the landing operations. One obscure admiral was so annoyed at being cheated of his chance for glory that he later publicly accused Miles of having exposed the Army to possible annihilation by moving into the interior without attacking San Juan.

The city of San Juan was densely populated. Any bombardment of the place would have resulted in wholesale killing of civilians, while the Spanish troops would have been relatively well protected within their fortifications. Such a deliberate slaughter and destruction would have been remembered and resented forever afterward, and Miles well knew it. In Cuba he had already foreseen the lasting distrust of Americans which would result from the bungled operations there—killing of rebel troops by mistake, the killing of some civilians, and widespread starvation and deprivation caused by the occupation.

But perhaps what motivated Miles more than the Cuban experience was the knowledge he had gained from all the years of studying the Indian nations—the lasting psychological aftermath of military operations involving primitive or underdeveloped cultures was an old story to him. With regard to the Puerto Rico campaign, in his written orders he stressed again and again the importance of *establishing and maintaining the friendship and respect* of the native population.

Miles issued strict directives, and he traveled around a good deal to see that they were carried out, to the effect that all local governments in every town or city were to be respected and aided when necessary. Currency was not to be devalued if possible. Supplies requisitioned were to be paid for fairly. At the same time, all Spanish troops and Spanish citizens were to be protected from mob violence and recriminations. Such American troop units as were not in action—and many were not—were kept busy building roads, communications, and other facilities that would aid the people in future development of the country.

When Miles left the island, hardly a month after he landed, he had created, in the eyes of the population at all levels, an image of the benevolent liberator. He had become a hero, a lasting symbol of the United States seldom, if ever, embodied in any other military leader in the whole course of our territorial expansion.

Unfortunately for the General, his popularity in Puerto Rico was not echoed in his own country on his return. No great parades and public acclamation greeted his arrival in New York, as had been bestowed on Dewey and other war celebrities. After all, he was only the commanding general of the United States Army. And thanks to the only news media, the press, most Americans didn't even know the post existed. The Administration was of no mind to educate them on this point. New York City officials, however, did put on a state dinner for Miles at the Waldorf. This would have been more gratifying had not Roosevelt used the occasion to make one of his rousing and colorful speeches, keeping the spotlight rather more on himself than on the general of the Army. The latter's public speeches were as formal and dull, we must admit after reading all that survive, as they were modest and impersonal.

One can imagine how Miles must have felt, though he did nothing to reveal it. At a dinner in his own honor, he was being elbowed aside, at least figuratively, by a mere lieutenant colonel, and a greenhorn volunteer at that. (Roosevelt had served under Col. Leonard Wood throughout the campaign.) Roosevelt had resigned from the Army the day he landed back in New York, losing no time in running for governor while his war exploits, both real and imaginary, were still in the public eye. To him the Miles dinner was a huge success.

It is perhaps pertinent to speculate briefly on the effect that Miles' "public image" was then having on the rest of his family. The thought comes to mind that this aspect of his life may also have had some bearing on the subsequent strange misinterpretation of his character by so many.

Mary's chief concern now was to keep her husband in the background of public affairs as much as possible. He was to be retired for age in 1903; until then Mary wanted only to maintain the status quo. During all the years of struggle for advancement she had battled with politicians, trying to get

217

her husband more recognition; now Miles was at the top of his military career. There was nowhere else to go except perhaps to enter the lists for some high public office. And Mary knew that he was anathema to many of the most powerful figures in both political parties. In a period of national enthusiasm for expansionism, they had him branded as an isolationist; an uncompromising troublemaker with outmoded ideals of behavior.

Mary's worst fear was that Miles might get involved in some sort of official investigation of the abuses of the recent war. He had already stated that he would favor such an investigation. Mary dreaded the social implications. Her main interest was in the impending engagement of Cecelia to a young West Point trained career officer, Maj. Samuel Reber, who had been with Miles in Puerto Rico. Sherman Miles was sixteen, an age at which he must have been acutely aware of his father's often shabby treatment by the Administration and the yellow journals. His only defense, which he was to maintain throughout his own later long career in the Army, was an attitude of extreme reticence and rigid impersonal reserve with regard to his father's reputation.

In spite of Mary's best efforts, Miles had been back in the States only a few days when he began to get into the thick of what became one of the stickiest and most notorious controversies in our national history. The deplorable condition of troops returning from Cuba, suffering by thousands from fever, food poisoning, and general debilitation—with hundreds already dead and thousands seriously ill—had suddenly become a national scandal. The newspapers, now that their enormously profitable exploitation of the war was ended, took up the situation with their usual irresponsible sensationalism. Headlines screamed demands for official investigations; the guilty parties must be smoked out and punished.

Most books covering this period, even those most favorable to Miles, give the impression that he plunged into this wrangle entirely of his own volition; and that he would have been much wiser, and much more respected in his later years, if he had kept out of it. To me it seems quite clear that had he remained silent, he would have fared worse in the end. With all the public clamor going on, he could not have prevented either the Administration or the Congress from launching some sort of investigation. Whoever in the War Department had been guilty of inefficiency or worse would be sure to try to pin some of the blame on the commanding general of the Army. Silence on the part of the latter would only be taken as an indication of either complicity or lack of courage.

However, Miles may have been ill advised and too little prepared with concrete evidence in his criticism of the War Department and his old nemesis, the Quartermaster Department, which still remained outside his command. He was soon being greatly encouraged and widely quoted by many so-called friends who were actually much more interested in discrediting the Administration than they were in anything that might happen to General Miles.

The main hue and cry centered around Miles' press interviews, in which he supported the claims of many officers and men that much of the illness in Cuba had been caused by chemically preserved canned beef and by refrigerated meats containing poisonous preservatives. The implication was that War Department appointees in charge of commissary supplies had been in collusion with the big meat-packers, and great profits had been made by selling the Army substandard rations. Headlines throughout the country named Miles as the author of charges concerning "poisoned meat" and "embalmed beef."

Democratic Congressmen soon responded to this publicity with loud demands for a congressional investigation. To forestall such an embarrassment to his regime, McKinley was forced to set up a board of inquiry himself, in the fall of 1898. A nine-man commission was named, loaded with members who could be counted on to protect the War Department and Secretary Alger, which in effect meant the strongest possible defense for McKinley himself.

I doubt if it would be possible today, even after wading through all the mountain of tangled testimony, and reading most of the subsequent writings on the subject, to come up with a very clear conclusion as to how justifiable the charges of collusion and graft really were. One does get an impression —all too clear—that this affair became one of the nastiest, most sordid, degrading, and dishonestly manipulated displays of dirty laundry in the history of U.S. government. (After this stage in my research was ended, it took me two or three days to regain a normal appetite for meat in any form.)

25

AS a key figure in this mess, Miles was trapped in a situation that brought him far more national attention in the newspapers than he had ever been accorded for his military accomplishments. As the whole controversy would never be solved or settled to anyone's satisfaction, it was to leave Miles forever afterward in the shadow of a murky cloud of suspicion, doubt, and acrimony raised by his Republican political enemies and yellow journals.

But in the earlier stages of the investigation, most of the press cast the General in the role of the fearless crusader who would stop at nothing to expose the villains who, for their own profit, had poisoned the heroic boys in his Army. And fearless he certainly was; for he was single-handedly tackling both the Administration and the rich and influential meat-packing combines.

At the same time Secretary of War Alger, whose popularity had slipped badly when the frightful condition of the returning troops became known, was held up by the newspapers as the chief culprit. There were widespread demands that if he would not resign, the President should dismiss him. But McKinley was much too loyal to his old political handyman to think of doing it.

The commission began by calling in a string of witnesses who had been in Cuba and were happy to swear that the tinned meat rations had been perfectly delicious, and the troops had relished every mouthful as though they were eating pâté de foie gras and caviar. Miles, however, aided by some of the newspaper correspondents and many of the most respected officers, was able to produce such an overwhelming amount of testimony to the contrary that even the loaded commission soon gave up its first approach. Instead the investigators decided a certain amount of meat spoilage, etc., had been inevitable—but not through any fault of the War Department or Alger. For a scapegoat they chose one Charles P. Egan, a regular Army general who had been attached to the commissary department.

Blaming his sudden plight, not unnaturally, entirely on Miles, Egan blew up before the commission and shouted so many insults at Miles that he was removed and charged with conduct unbecoming an officer. This was followed by a court-martial and suspension from the Army. Meanwhile the commission examined Alger and pronounced him entirely innocent of any laxity or complicity in the matter of the Army meat supplies. A finding that might have been expected, as the members of the commission from the outset had been so flattering to the Secretary as to address him as "General Alger" even though he was of course a civilian official.

Knowing well that the commission's real purpose was to shield Alger from further embarrassing exposures and to discredit Miles' testimony, the general of the Army refused to be sworn as a witness. His excuse was that it was not proper for such a commission to investigate a matter that should come within the province of the Army; and that he should be allowed to conduct the investigation himself. His plan certainly had more merit than the one being followed, but of course McKinley had no intention of considering it.

Miles, however, had stirred up such a furor that the public at large was not convinced by the commission's decision that the Army meat supplies had been simon pure except for some spoilage caused by tropical heat. The papers began editorializing about the "whitewash commission," and Alger was more unpopular than ever. McKinley decided something must be done to quiet things down, so he appointed a military court of inquiry as Miles had demanded—with the slight difference that it did not include Miles and consisted of three officers of the President's choice.

This time it was found that the canned meat had indeed been unfit to eat, but not because of the content; only because supplies in Cuba had been kept too long in improper storage conditions before being opened. The crowning irony was the further decision that Miles should be reprimanded for not having informed the War Department, when he reached Puerto Rico, that the meat rations were unacceptable! (Conveniently ignored were the facts that Miles had not been allowed to go to Cuba, where most of the suffering and sickness had occurred, until almost the end of the campaign; that he had long pleaded to have the supply departments placed under his command; and that actually he had sent reams of complaints about the Army rations and other deficiencies of supply, most of which had brought no action whatever from the War Department.)

No action was taken on the findings of the military inquiry, and the great "embalmed beef" scandal, having dragged on for several months, began to disappear from the news. If, as Miles had always believed, there had been flagrant graft and corruption in the dealings between the War Department's bureau of commissary supply and the meat-packers, no one was ever exposed or punished, except for the unfortunate Egan. Many of Miles' witnesses had not been heard, and others discredited. He himself would undoubtedly have been relieved of his command by McKinley but for his great popularity within the Army and among most of the high-ranking generals.

Miles had been beaten, but he had given the Administration and Alger such a hard time that the latter found it expedient to resign shortly afterward. Most unfortunate for Miles was the lasting effect the affair was to have on the press. In those days the newspapers loved a winner. Miles had been unable to produce the culprits of the meat scandal who would have made such good copy. And the press, forever afterward, would see that he was rewarded either by slanted references or by being ignored entirely.

To assess the great part played by the newspapers in Miles' subsequent neglect as a national celebrity, it is essential to delve somewhat into the character of the press at the turn of the century. For the press of that time was vastly different from that of later years with which we are more familiar. It was a time when newspapers had reached a peak of power and influence comparable, in terms of the present, to the combined effects of television news, radio news, news magazines, and papers themselves, all in one package. But while all the modern media are controlled by many restraints, both legal and ethical, there were no such restraints on newspapers at the height of their power. Almost anything could be printed that would tempt people to buy more papers.

A few dominant newspaper magnates had more influence, both at large and on the government, than the titans of manufacturing and railroads; they could even compete with the Wall Street bankers. William Randolph Hearst boasted that his papers had "made" the Spanish-American War, and he later used them to promote himself for President. The first Joseph Pulitzer was fond of telling his associates he had sufficient influence to make or break, at will, any Presidential candidate who might be up for election. The news barons didn't need to seek interviews with Presidents, kings, and dictators; the heads of state of the Western world came to see *them*.

Pulitzer was a self-educated eccentric with a genius for making money, both from his papers and from the stock market. His total income was never made public, but it is known to have been well over a million dollars a year at one time (of course, equal to many times that today). If he heard that some department in one of his papers was losing a few dollars he would get insomnia and lie awake all night. As he traveled about the world, he was constantly dictating to six or seven private secretaries and sending endless directives to his editors. The messages always ended with the same admonition—his employees should always keep in mind that the success of the papers was much more important than the salaries they were being paid. He was able to hire the best journalists of his time, but could seldom keep them long.

Pulitzer's original stake came from building up his two papers in St. Louis; they were soon known as the most infamous, sensational, and irresponsible in the whole Midwest—and consequently among the most lucrative. He then acquired the New York *World* and proceeded to develop it along such opposite lines that it became New York's leading crusading paper, dedicated to all sorts of reforms, with unequaled influence in the country at large. It was as though Pulitzer was driven day and night, at the cost of his health and much of his vast wealth, to make himself feel accepted by the highest echelons of society and by intellectual leaders both here and abroad. But though enormously successful in attaining almost every ambition, he seemed incapable of ever feeling secure or satisfied.

Hearst was a much less complex character. As a young man, in the 1890's, he bought the New York *Journal* and challenged Pulitzer's *World* to a circulation duel. It lasted for years. The older man was sure Hearst would run out of money; but even after losing some eight million dollars, Hearst was still able to get more backing from his mother, the widow of a wealthy California financier. Finally Pulitzer gave up the fight and it ended in a stalemate. From that time on, Hearst began to expand his chain and rapidly recouped the money he had lost.

Most large papers, except for Villard's liberal *Post*, were violently partisan and biased to a degree that the next generation would not have tolerated and that today could only seem ludicrous. (A *Journal* editorial once seriously suggested that somebody should be found to shoot President McKinley; though this had no connection with his later assassination.)

The power of the press was shown in the rise and fall of the fortunes of Admiral George Dewey, the national hero of 1898. After Manila, Dewey was deified by the public in a manner not equaled until Lindbergh flew the Atlantic. The Dewey name was used to promote everything from the sale of sheet music to chewing gum. If Dewey walked down the street to get his white moustache trimmed, the event would make the front pages.

The Democratic party, looking for a man who might beat McKinley, approached Dewey in the fall of 1898. The Admiral expressed no interest whatever, saying he knew nothing about politics or government. The newspapers soon dropped the matter, but the following spring Dewey suddenly announced to a single newspaper reporter, at a casual interview, that he had decided to run for the Presidency. When this scoop appeared in the headlines of the paper for whom the reporter worked, all the rest of the national press was furious that no general release had been issued. Dewey was at once besieged by reporters from everywhere, and on being asked which party he planned to represent, he replied that he had not yet made up his mind. This was more than enough for the reporters. At that time, in contrast to the vastly different time in which something of the same nature was said of Eisenhower, for a man to admit he had no commitment to a particular party was as bad as saying he had no religious convictions.

The papers, both Democratic and Republican, went to work on Dewey. Stories came out claiming the admiral had said his ambitious wife had persuaded him to run. Later, that he had denied it. He was quoted as saying he had made up for his earlier ignorance of politics and lack of experience by reading the papers all winter, and was now quite well enough informed to serve as President. And finally, that he had decided he was a Democrat. In a couple of weeks the beloved national celebrity had become a laughingstock. Far from getting the nomination, he could not have been elected fence viewer in any town in the land.

It should be added, however, that almost any publicity, in terms of long-range historical importance, is better than none. Over the years historians and biographers have managed to restore Dewey pretty much to his original statue as one of our great naval heroes. He has fared far better, at any rate, than his contemporary, the general of the Army.

26

MILES was given only sporadic attention by the press during the three years following the "embalmed beef" dramatization. Fighting in the Philippines dragged on; much of the population there had not been told, apparently, that after the armistice with Spain, McKinley had persuaded Congress to annex the whole archipelago as a territory of the United States. Nobody in America seems to have gotten the message that the *insurrectos,* or nationalists, were quite sure to go on fighting us for the next forty-eight years, just as they had fought the Spaniards before us.

But war news is made at the front, not in a Washington Army headquarters office, especially if the commanding general in that office has no part in the making or carrying out of military policy and decisions. The General was back where he had been before the war with Spain—kept confined to purely routine matters. The President, through the War Department, dictated whatever orders were given to the commanders in the Philippines.

In January of 1900 Cecelia Miles was married to Maj. Samuel Reber, the handsome and popular West Point graduate, class of 1886. The splendor of that wedding, with its prominent attendance both military and social, was reminiscent of her parents' own, when Mary's Uncle Cump occupied the same post the bride's father now held. The bridegroom was the one man in the world who would be most pleasing to the General. Reber had become an electrical engineer and a pioneer in developing new techniques in the signal corps, one of Miles' own pet enthusiasms ever since his early work with heliographs. Reber was also a cavalryman and sufficiently expert in horsemanship to pass muster with his father-in-law.

By mid-1901, Miles had refrained from badgering the War Department for so long it was finally decided he should receive some special recognition. The long unused rank of lieutenant general was revived and officially conferred on him. Perhaps the new Secretary of War, Elihu Root, felt the honor would tend to keep Miles in a benevolent state of mind. In any case, the title did not convey one whit more authority than he had been allowed previously. (The rank of lieutenant general *should* have been a clue for later historians to Miles' military importance—it had been held after the Civil War by Sherman, Sheridan, and Schofield, in that order. Miles had still been ranked as a major general though designated as commanding general of the army. This has often been confused with the *rank* called general of the Army which rates above the rank of lieutenant general. But in Miles' time "general of the Army" was not used to denote an actual rank.)

Miles was unable to intimidate Root into giving him a more active part in directing the activities of Army units abroad, as he had for a time at least been able to intimidate Alger. Then, on September 4, 1901, with the death of President McKinley by assassination, Vice-President Roosevelt was inaugurated and hence also became commander-in-chief of the U.S. military forces. Nothing could have more surely predetermined that the general of the Army, in his last active year, would have an extremely poor chance of winning any further distinctions.

By this time, mere mention of Miles reminded the new President of an unending chain of grievances. During the war the General had ignored his noisy efforts to publicize his rather unrealistic version of the role played by the Rough Riders regiment. Then Miles had become an inflexible and outspoken critic of the expansionist policy Roosevelt fostered with near religious fervor. He had also vocally opposed Roosevelt's concept of a general staff system, among many other differences of opinion.

It seems to me there was also a factor of personal jealousy involved. Roosevelt had the stature of certain greatness as a statesman, attested to by great accomplishments in certain fields, and he had enormous energy and mental ability. But he was also a man of almost uncontrollable appetites: a craving, after his sickly youth, for renown in the "manly sports," which he satisfied by shooting elephants and lions; a craving for rich foods, which kept him overweight; a craving for personal popularity, for constant applause, perhaps as a compensation for his almost grotesque lack of physical charms. In contrast, Miles was the beau ideal in build and features, a giant of physical fitness in any company, a natural sportsman and athlete; his very manner, personally reticent, always dignified, as though incapable of courting any form of favor, must have been irritating to the impulsive and opportunistic Roosevelt.

I could find no record that Miles himself ever acknowledged, in private or in public, Roosevelt's bitter enmity toward him. (In his later memoirs he did not even mention Roosevelt.) Nor did he make any concessions or overtures, now that Roosevelt was President. Even at an early age he had not been one to stand in awe of superiors under any conditions. At age sixty-three, robust and full of drive as ever, well aware that he was the top military man of his country—in experience and accomplishments and rank, if not in actual authority—he was of no mind to sit around, whenever he had something to say, waiting for permission from Root or Roosevelt.

An occasion soon arose. In December a naval court of inquiry finally got around to deciding whether Admiral Schley or Admiral Sampson had been in the right, in the old controversy over who should get the credit for winning the Battle of Santiago in 1898. Today it is hard to believe that this ludicrously unwarranted affair could have been taken seriously by the government or the public.

The inquiry was requested by Schley himself (which would seem a strong indication he was guiltless) after the appearance of a naval history by E. S. Maclay, stating that Schley was a "caitiff, poltroon, and coward" and fabricating a damning account of his conduct in the battle of Santiago. It appeared that Maclay had done this in an effort to uphold Sampson's old claim that he alone had been in command of the fleet and hence solely responsible for the victory, absurd and utterly untenable though it was, in light of his complete absence from the battle. Whether or not Sampson may have fed the story to Maclay, he had read the proofs of it and approved them.

Schley's long record of service was outstanding, including a world-famous daring rescue of the explorer Adolphus Greely from Arctic ice floes in 1884. He was confident an inquiry would clear him of the scurrilous charges published in the Maclay history and permit him to take some appropriate action. But he underestimated Sampson's lasting jealous animosity and the extent of his influence.

Admiral Dewey was appointed to the three-man board to give it the best possible window dressing. The honest, if politically naïve, Dewey was anxious to serve because he was horrified at the thought of Schley's being cheated of proper credit for Santiago and even accused of misconduct in that battle. But the two other officers were carefully chosen Sampson men, and they voted against Schley on every count, paying no more attention to the mass of official reports and documents offered in Schley's defense than if they had been so much blank paper.

Evidence had been dug up and embellished by Sampson supporters, to the effect that Schley, in the dense smoke of the bombardment of the Spanish fleet, had given an order to his helmsman to turn his ship in an arc that could have resulted in collision with one of the other ships. On this three-year-old scuttlebutt, and nothing else in the way of evidence, the two Sampson men—admirals Benham and Ramsay—found Schley guilty of "vacillation, lack of enterprise, and disobedience."

Dewey's finding was for total vindication—with high praise for Schley's prompt and efficient action, and full credit for his having destroyed the Spanish fleet. But it may be remembered that the newspapers, before this, had largely destroyed Dewey's popularity, and hence his credibility. The inquiry's verdict was officially declared a "disagreement," but the two-against-one vote could not fail to ruin Schley's career and leave a permanent and very damaging blight on his reputation.

Schley at once filed an appeal with the Secretary of the Navy, John Davis Long, the notorious bungler of Spanish-American War days who was still in office. Long upheld the decision and refused to consider the appeal. Schley's last resort to any vestiges of justice that might still exist was a direct appeal to the President. Roosevelt, however, only chose to approve the findings of Long, for no other apparent reason than to avoid alienating a few of his political friends. This act would seem to have set an all-time record for the most vicious, unwarranted, cowardly, and selfishly motivated public character assassination ever sanctioned by a United States President.

General Miles' reaction to the news of the majority verdict was immediate, violent, and loudly vocal, to the dismay of his wife and many of his friends. Before long, a swarm of reporters began happily sending the newspapers various versions of his remarks. As Miles saw it, Dewey was the only member of the board of inquiry who had been thoroughly qualified to pass judgment. The other two had obviously been appointed because they could be counted on in advance to support Sampson's trumped-up claims. The only shred of evidence that had been proved against Schley was that he had indeed given an order to turn his ship, in the dense smoke, toward a sister ship. But the latter's officers had been able to see Schley's ship in time to veer off, and no harm had been done. Hardly a cause for a naval court of inquiry to destroy the character and reputation of a man whose long career had been a model of accomplishments and integrity!

Miles felt that there was no law or rule of ethics to prevent him from speaking out for justice. After all, he had no connection with the Navy. He was as much entitled to the rights of free speech as any other citizen, so long as he didn't break any Army regulation. But, of course, the consensus of "establishment" thinking hardly agreed with him on this point, as would doubtless be equally true today. The General was soon informed that Roosevelt was so annoyed he was considering the most extreme retribution possible for such a breach of propriety—an official reprimand.

To carry out the threat, however, was evidently beyond the nerve even of the fiery, arrogant Roosevelt. But when Miles went to the White House, hoping that the President would listen to his side of the argument, Roosevelt, in the presence of various witnesses, angrily called the General to task for having publicly supported Schley and then dismissed him.

And thus the affair was ended, except for the interesting things that happened to that little phrase "official reprimand," as it was rediscovered from time to time by later researchers poring over the garbled accounts in old newspaper files. What had begun as a hearsay rumor that Roosevelt had "considered" an official reprimand began to be altered into the flat statement that Roosevelt had indeed "reprimanded" Miles. Naturally, this carried with it the assumption that Miles must in some way have merited such a reprimand. By 1910, the legend showed up in *Everybody's Encyclopedia,* which stated that Miles had publicly defended Dewey's report on Schley "and was reprimanded therefore." In more recent years, other encyclopedias have expanded this into a seemingly factual statement to the effect that in December, 1901, President Roosevelt sent an official reprimand to General Miles.

And so, once more, we have found Miles' record indelibly blemished, on evidence that is little more than fantasy. With his usual reckless disregard for his own reputation, Miles had stood up for Admiral Schley, one of the most wronged men of his time, when almost no one else in any position of prominence had dared raise a voice. You can find his reward today in many standard encyclopedias—the "official reprimand" story.

I am reminded again of the book *In the Days of McKinley* and its last reference to Miles, in an account of the Army beef investigation. This version is the most unsavory one I have yet run across. According to Margaret Leech, Miles was filled with frustration because the armistice had prevented his winning glory on the battlefield in Puerto Rico. So he dreamed up the beef investigation for the sole purpose of gaining publicity to further his burning political ambitions.

During 1902 Miles continued to annoy the President and Secretary of War by insisting that the fighting in the Philippines should, and could, be brought to an end. He was sure that if he were allowed to go to Manila and take command in person, he could arrange an armistice, employing the same principles he had used so successfully in Puerto Rico. He prepared a detailed plan of his proposed action and submitted it to the War Department. Secretary Root sent the plan along to Roosevelt, together with his own curt conclusion that Miles was entirely out of order and trying to interfere with the affairs of state. The President's only comment was that Root's views were entirely approved.

Miles had not yet realized how vastly different from his own were both the motives and the ultimate aims of Roosevelt, Root, and their supporters, with regard to the Philippines campaign. Miles still thought the long-range objective was what had originally been projected to Congress and the public at large—to retain bases and to aid the Filipino people in governing themselves in a democratic manner that would insure lasting ties with the United States. But Roosevelt saw himself as the first great promoter of worldwide territorial expansion, in which the permanent acquisition of the Philippines was an important step. He had no belief in any "inferior" peoples' ability (or rights, for that matter) to govern themselves. A patrician racist at heart, back in his gentleman-rancher days on the frontier he had hoped to be able to shoot an Indian or two himself. (Only if they were trespassing on his land, of course.)

The Roosevelt-Root thinking was that we must wipe out these *insurrectos,* which should certainly not take longer than several months. After all, it was a case of a well-equipped modern army against an ill-armed ignorant crowd of barefoot natives. As for the *insurrecto* leaders, just get rid of them, they're all traitors anyway. Any attempt at negotiation with these treacherous people would of course be useless. The mass of the population would quite naturally see the futility of supporting the *insurrectos* and welcome the benefits of American occupation.

The American officers chosen to command the expeditionary forces in the Philippines played their part well. Their dispatches contained the information that the great majority of the Filipino people were not really supporting the *insurrectos,* except when the latter's atrocities frightened them into it. Of course it was a nasty war, and casualties were sometimes heavy, because the *insurrectos* didn't fight at all fairly—they often used knives instead of guns, and they sneaked up through the grass at night to attack American outposts and then retreated in a cowardly fashion back into impenetrable jungles. But just send us a few thousand more men, and we'll whip them before next Christmas. There are no doubts out here among the officers and the boys in the lines that we are winning this war. We have established very good relations with the Filipino people, except for the minority of fanatical nationalists who are persisting in their hopeless guerilla tactics against us. The *insurrectos* cannot long sustain such heavy losses, and already there are definite signs that they are becoming seriously weakened in several areas.

If in all this there is detected any slight resemblance to events during the first year or so of the war in Vietnam, it is strictly accidental and was not my objective. I am only condensing here what can be found in any well-documented book dealing with the warfare in the Philippines, or in the military records of that campaign.

27

TOTAL American forces in the Philippines in 1902 were some fifty thousand men, a great many more than had been in action throughout the war with Spain. Yet public interest here at home about what was going on in the Philippines was relatively slight, considerably less than the public interest taken in the Korean War in 1950. Miles himself could not obtain half as much information as he would have liked.

News by cablegram was extremely limited, and of course subject to strict military censorship. All other news dispatches took weeks to reach the United States. Published accounts of fighting in the Philippines had the lively flavor of a bottle of beer that had been uncapped and left in the refrigerator for a month before being discovered. In magazines there were frequent stories of American heroism and native atrocities, but these were apt to be more or less fictional, whether or not they were so labeled. When reread today, the fictional effect seems heightened by the illustrations—usually drawn by some New York artist whose conception of Philippine scenery looks like the Jersey meadows studded with palm trees. The natives all resemble Australian aborigines, in contrast to the stalwart Boy Scout appearance of the Americans.

To the average American of that time, including the typical Congressman or newspaper editor, the extent of the military involvement that would be necessary if we were to control these far-off Pacific islands was as little understood as why Filipino began with *F* and Philippines with *Ph*. But there was almost no dissent from any quarter. It would have been considered legal grounds for insanity had any military expert predicted that fighting might still be going on, some day, between grandsons of those crazy Filipino nationalists and grandsons of our own boys out there.

By late summer of 1902 Miles realized he had exactly twelve months of active duty left before reaching retirement age. The thought of spending his last year in the position of a figurehead at a Washington desk, with his only knowledge of the continued fighting in the Philippines doled out second-hand by the dictatorial and hostile Secretary of War, was almost intolerable. As urgently as he could, Miles again requested the necessary orders to allow him to go to the Philippines.

This time Elihu Root met the request with a proposition that may have been inspired by Roosevelt; in any case Roosevelt approved it. Miles was to go on a round-the-world inspection tour of American bases and was also to observe military conditions in Japan, China, and Russia. Thus the time allotted to the Philippines would allow only a short stop there. The commanding officers on the scene were alerted so that they could show him only what they wanted him to see, and he would be on his way before he had time to make any embarrassing reports. He was not to issue any orders, merely to observe. The plan backfired disastrously for the Administration. As a result, the increased antagonism toward Miles would make his previous status look almost favored.

It began when the General reached the base at Guam and made his inspection. As Root should have known, to Miles an inspection did not mean sitting in the shade with the top brass and watching some selected troops pass by in review. Among other things, Miles soon discovered that some Filipinos were being confined on Guam, and among them was Apolonario Mabine, who had been Secretary of State of the Philippine Republic when the U.S. Army had taken over. Miles insisted on an interview with the former Filipino statesman.

After the talk with Mabine, the General sent an emphatic and detailed report to Washington urging his release. Miles said that Mabine had no knowledge of why he was being confined in such a remote exile, under heavy guard, apparently for the rest of his life. He was in such poor health, paralyzed and emaciated, he had to be carried out of his miserable cell and propped up in a chair. It seemed plain that, as he had remarked, he "could do the United States no harm"; except that if he were allowed to die in a military prison, he might become a martyr and inspire the Filipino *insurrectos* to still greater efforts against United States rule. Hoping that his report would produce some action (it did not, until he returned to Washington and vigorously followed it up), Miles went on to Manila.

Though he had been instructed by Root not to "interfere" in any way with the command in the Philippines, there is no record that Miles agreed explicitly to comply. On the other hand, he must certainly have been astute enough to know that if he voiced any disagreement he would never have been allowed to make the trip. In any case, all went well at first. He found the troops to be generally in good order, well equipped and well disciplined, and morale seemed high at all the encampments.

Then, at some point along the way, his escort being unable to divert him from a keen questioning of all and sundry, civilian and military, Miles began to pick up some very disquieting rumors. It was common talk among Filipinos, it seemed, that some American officers were making a practice of torturing *insurrecto* prisoners to obtain military information, using such tactics as pumping them full of water with pressurized hoses. Those who refused to talk did not always survive these persuasions.

Now the fat was in the fire! To the unbounded displeasure of the commanders at headquarters, their visiting superior insisted on riding out from their luxurious suburban villas and inspecting certain well-sequestered areas where prisoners were confined.

It was these Army prison compounds, by the way, and not the later ones in Europe, which first gave rise to the use of the term "concentration camp." In Cuba the U.S. troops had become familiar with the notorious prison camps set up by the Spaniards, and in fact one of the avowed purposes of the campaign had been to eliminate them. The nationalists who had been confined in these camps were called *concentrados*. Some of the same officers who had fought to free the Cubans from these hellholes were now found to be setting up the same sort of brutal enclosures, which they called concentration camps, in the undeclared war against the Filipino nationalists.

It was the age-old theory of retaliation in kind which always crops up in a war of long duration. The Filipino nationalists had not conformed to the American rules of conduct in war. They had committed atrocities. And anyway they were not really legitimate enemies—they were traitors, not only to their new benevolent rulers, the Americans, but to all their own *good* people who were collaborating with the Americans.

Miles had never tolerated this theory in his own commands back in the Indian fighting years. He was not going to tolerate it now, in any part of the Army, if he could prevent it. He sat down and wrote out orders to all U.S. commanders in the Philippines. There was to be no more torturing of prisoners. All *insurrectos* captured were to be treated strictly according to the rules and regulations governing the rights of prisoners of war.

When news of Miles' action reached Washington both the Administration and the War Department were so badly upset they made every effort to discredit him. He had exceeded his authority. He had been directed not to issue any orders, but no sooner had he landed in the Philippines than he began to badger the commanders there and impede them in the performance of their duties. It is significant that he was not recalled from his journey; apparently the farther away from Washington he was the better, until this mess could be smoothed over.

Miles felt he was justified on two counts. As long as he was still the commanding general of the Army, the War Department had had no clearly defined grounds for depriving him of all authority. He had not interfered in any tactical matters, but had issued orders only to correct a flagrant violation of Army regulations. In *Serving the Republic*, Miles refers to the incident and defends himself with the single sentence, "I would rather that any official act of my life might be erased than to have omitted discharging a duty that was prompted by a sense of justice and humanity, to preserve the good name of our army."

The only trouble with this credo, then and perhaps always, was that the great majority of those in high places believed the best way to preserve the good name of the Army, whenever some irregularity was discovered, was to sweep it under the rug as quietly as possible. Serenely undisturbed by the enormous furor his "sense of justice" was stirring up in the government and in the national press at home, Miles embarked for Japan.

At first Administration spokesmen tried to counteract the publicity given by the newspapers to the brutal treatment of Filipino prisoners. But their credibility was severely weakened by one circumstance—the original disclosures had come from the commanding general of the Army himself; he might be discredited in other respects, but nobody had ever had much luck trying to impugn his well-known reputation for blunt truthfulness and damn the consequences.

From this distance in time, even after reading quite ambitiously on the subject, one finds it hard to assess the extent of what had happened in the Philippines. But it seems certain there were at least several instances of unwarranted brutality, and that some deaths were directly attributable to interrogation methods. At any rate, Miles' action did force the War Department to make an investigation of its own which confirmed this, and to take positive steps toward ending the practices which had previously not been acknowledged.

Roosevelt, throughout his two terms, would keep the government firmly and aggressively committed to his theory that all Filipino nationalists could, and must, be thoroughly whipped by U.S. military power. The American people believed this had in fact been accomplished in 1901, when General Frederick Funston put down the first revolt and captured its leader, Emilio Aguinaldo. But following Aguinaldo's defeat, there came an endless succession of nationalist leaders to keep up the challenge to United States occupancy of what they considered their own sovereign country. Time after time, over the years, the Army "crushed" the nationalists and "ended" Filipino resistance. Actually the United States had no more chance of subjugating the Filipino nationalists, in half a century of occupation, than the French were to have in their long and tragic struggle to retain control in Vietnam.

It now seems amazing that Roosevelt could have so thoroughly convinced just about all the American people that United States power simply could not fail to stamp out all resistance in the Philippines. We would remain convinced until after World War II, when our vast involvement elsewhere in Asia and our preoccupation with blocking the spread of Communism made it seem expedient to grant independence. It was realized at last that a friendly independent ally was preferable to a troublesome U.S. territory in a more or less permanent state of revolt.

If we acknowledge that Roosevelt's Philippine policy was supported by nearly 100 percent of public opinion, it follows that Miles' views must have been rejected to an equal extent. Eventually, half the American public would come around to Miles' way of thinking (and half of the Western world too, for that matter) on such matters as racial minorities, colonialism, and the rights of small nations; but all Americans, by that time, would have quite forgotten our first military leader to have propounded such ideas publicly.

The General's opinion, which was to add very considerably to his status as a candidate for oblivion, is shown in some reflections on his inspection tour of the Philippines, written some years afterward while working on his book *Serving the Republic*.

> The Filipinos are a quiet, industrious, polite people. Many of the better class are college bred; and as for their qualifications for self-government, they have furnished men in great numbers to exercise the duties of civil government in all the various positions from Secretary of State, judges, governors of the principalities, presidents of the municipal governments, down to the more subordinate positions, both *before* [italics mine] and since our occupation, and in my judgement the sooner we allow them to establish a government that would be for their benefit as well as ours, both in close diplomatic and commercial interests, the sooner we will have the glory of having established the first republic in the orient.

Ideas of this sort would have stirred up little interest even if they had been presented in less ponderous and jumbo-sized sentences. It is not surprising to find that when the book appeared in 1911 it enjoyed an immediate and almost total lack of success.

It is characteristic of Miles' dry military-report style of writing that he condenses, in a couple of pages, his account of what must have been one of the most colorful and exciting trips imaginable.

From the Philippine Islands I went to Hong-Kong and Canton, China, and thence to Japan. From Nagasaki I went to Port Arthur, where I was received by Admiral Alexeieff, commanding the Russian military and naval forces. He stated that he had at that time eighty thousand men under his command, and from my conversation with the Russian officers I concluded that they were anticipating war with Japan. From there I went to Tientsin and Peking, where I was granted an audience by the Empress Dowager, whom I found a most interesting character and one of the remarkable sovereigns of the world. During her reign she brought about many reforms, such as the prohibition of torture, the discouragement of the importation of opium, measures for a constitutional government and a parliament, and for the encouragement of education.

On leaving Peking I passed over northern China, Manchuria, via the Trans-Siberian Road to Moscow and St. Petersburg. The journey in midwinter was one of the most interesting of my life, as it enabled me to compare that sparsely settled, vast area of country with our Western country. It is much greater in extent, better timbered, well watered, with an abundance of natural resources, very little mountainous country, and the zone passed over would compare favorably, as far as climate is concerned, with our own temperate or middle zone. At St. Petersburg, in a conversation with the War Minister of the Russian Empire, he informed me that the army was then composed of 1,700,000, and with their reserves they could increase their strength to 4,000,000. They were evidently anticipating war with Japan, but at no time during that war did they ever utilize any great portion of their military power.

On arriving at Paris, I received an invitation to visit Windsor Castle, England, and was the guest of King Edward, whom I had met before, and whom I regarded as one of the strongest as well as one of the most gracious sovereigns of the world.

I returned to Washington on the 1st of February, 1903.

The narrative of the book, by the way, ends right there. It is followed by a tedious and formal message to the Army on his retirement, written in the third person—General Orders, No. 116, dated August 5, 1903. An appendix contains a lengthy article on the potentials of irrigation in the West, written for the magazine *North American Review* in 1890.

28

ON arriving home from his round the world tour, the General was absorbed with the fact that he was the last Army commander under the old system. In six months, at his retirement, the newly organized General Staff would take over. There was nothing whatever he could do about this, as the plan had long been approved and was in the final stages of preparation. However, he refused to lend his approval to the plan, and continued to criticize it openly whenever asked for an opinion.

For refusing to budge from this stand, Miles was branded by the Administration, by the newer elements in the military establishment, and by many newspapers as a reactionary whose thinking was entirely outmoded. At least that was among the more polite descriptions applied to him. The image has stuck firmly to his memory ever since—the man who opposed the General Staff, opposed the modernization of the Army; the man who became a has-been before he was retired. But after digging back into this distinctly dull and uninspiring matter in some detail, it seems to me that Miles was not so much opposed to the concept of a General Staff as he was to the manner in which it was conceived and was being carried out.

Miles believed, as did General Douglas MacArthur so much later on, that the commanding general in any action should have a voice in the policy-making concerned with the action.

He would be remembered for his opposition to a General Staff system but forgotten as the first advocate of a great many changes the staff system was supposed to achieve, such as the unification of the supply departments under the overall command of the Army. Miles wanted something like a general staff, but still under the command of the top-ranking general. The new plan, he felt, was designed to make the high command much more subservient to the control of the civilian administrative branch of the government than he liked, and make the highest officers vulnerable to political favoritism.

It will only be remarked here that the rather pitiful condition of the Army at the outset of World War I indicated that Miles had been right, at least to the extent that the new system would not cure all the old evils. (To mention just one example, the infantry even then was not mechanized; he had recommended, back in 1902, that it should be.)

In the spring of 1903, Roosevelt proposed a quaint scheme for testing the fitness of aging Army officers. The suggestion had more publicity value than practical use, as the President himself may have realized. The idea was that any officer who could not ride a horse ninety miles in three days should retire from active duty. Miles had only about a month left before he would be retired anyway, at the mandatory age of sixty-four; but this was too good a chance to pass up. It would be his last chance to make Roosevelt look ridiculous.

The General announced at once that he would try the test himself. He laid out a course between Fort Sill and Fort Reno, Oklahoma, and had fresh horses posted every ten miles. Early one morning, he swung into the saddle of mount number one and cantered off across the prairie. Probably he didn't even need a compass; he had traveled the same route often during the Kiowa-Comanche uprising of 1874. Around midafternoon he trotted briskly up to a waiting crowd at the end of the course, showing no sign of any great fatigue. According to the newspaper accounts of the trip which appeared the next day, his time for the ninety miles had been checked at nine and a half hours.

I am truly sorry I can find no record of any comment by Roosevelt when he heard the news of the General's remarkable ride. Maybe he just snorted and made some remark about that proud old peacock—a term he had once before been heard to apply to Miles.

On the day of Miles' official retirement there were the customary formalities at the War Department, with one very notable omission—neither the President nor his Secretary of War were heard from. Though this fact may not seem of any special importance at first glance, it has given writers and historians ever since one more excuse for paying such scant and misguided attention to Miles. Roosevelt and Root had no cause to love Miles while he was still active, certainly. But to ignore him now that he could no longer trouble them—to refuse to bestow customary citations at his retirement, to refuse him even the dignity of a formal note of congratulations written by a Presidential secretary—*this* was a breach of official courtesy without parallel, in similar circumstances, in the term of any other United States President before or since.

Though kindness, or even courtesy, to anyone who had ever opposed him was not one of Roosevelt's prominent traits, he would go down in history as a President of many undeniably great accomplishments—the Panama Canal, trust-busting, conservation, and more. Among the military, Roosevelt would be remembered as the man who instituted the General Staff system, while Miles would be remembered (or perhaps more accurately, nearly forgotten) as the man who opposed it. The fact alone that Roosevelt so despised Miles, as shown by his refusal to grant any token of honor on the General's retirement, would convince all Roosevelt admirers forever afterward that Miles must have deserved such treatment. They would never try to find out what kind of man Miles really was, or what his real accomplishments had been in terms of military history.

The death of Mary Miles, a year after the General retired, probably had a great deal to do with his subsequent withdrawal from the public scene. For thirty-six years he had been able to rely on her support in every major decision of his life. He was, of course, about the last person to make any show of grief, even in his private life; so this is still largely a matter of deduction.

Anxious to find any change of scene that would occupy his mind, Miles accepted an offer to head the Massachusetts state militia. In this capacity he spent much of the time for the next three or four years back in his native state. But the job proved more honorary than active. Occasional efforts at making various changes and improvements in the militia were not very rewarding, and he finally decided to resign.

He returned to his Washington home, but it depressed him because of its spacious emptiness, and he soon bought a smaller one. Before long this too began to bother him, and he moved permanently into an apartment at the Rochambeau, a Washington hostelry of quiet luxury.

It would not be discovered until the future age of television that retired high-ranking generals, however ancient and out of touch, could be used to good advantage whenever a gap in a news program needed to be filled. In this respect Miles could have topped the field. His theatrically handsome features, erect bearing, and keenly alert manner changed remarkably little up to the time of his death at eighty-five, according to those who best remember him.

When the United States entered the First World War in 1917, the name of Nelson A. Miles again became associated with that of Theodore Roosevelt in a manner both humorous and somewhat tragic. By this time Roosevelt had also been retired for some years. At almost the same time, both men tendered their services to President Wilson, hoping quite seriously to be given some active military position. Both were politely refused. Though it apparently went unnoticed by the press, the only general officer in American military history to have served in three wars—Civil War, Indian campaigns, Spanish-American—was eager and ready to serve in a fourth, World War I. (What a pity Wilson did not have the imagination to give Miles even some job of little consequence, for a brief time, just for the record!)

By the end of the war Miles had long made his peace with obscurity. He was much more interested in the successfully developing careers of his son and son-in-law. Both earned enough distinction in World War I to afford even Miles, with his somewhat archaic ideals of military performance, considerable pride and satisfaction. Sherman Miles was well on his way toward the eventual rank of major general. Samuel Reber left the service after the war with the rank of colonel; but as he quickly became one of the powers in the development of the Radio Corporation of America, putting away his uniform probably caused his father-in-law little disappointment.

It would be nice to spin out at some length an interesting story of the last ten years of Miles' life. But such material as exists could only be developed into some sort of conjectural and perhaps sentimental reconstruction, which would not shed any further true light on the General's importance in history or why he was allowed to become so largely forgotten. So we have only the picture of an old gentleman living quietly in his Washington apartment, playing chess, at which he had long been an expert, and trying to teach the finer points of the game to his grandchildren when they came to visit. Miles did not grow very infirm with age, and he continued to ride his horses regularly until, in his final years, he was persuaded to take up driving them instead. Still the ardent traveler, he took several tours abroad. In autumn he liked to take his dogs and with some old friend go West to shoot on his old hunting grounds. He also became an enthusiastic golfer.

Miles always liked entertainment of an active, outdoor sort —rodeos, horse shows and races, parades and marching bands, circuses. The still popular Wild West shows, which had been originated by Buffalo Bill Cody, probably brought back amusing memories of his old friend. In the spring of 1925, at a Washington performance of the Ringling Circus, Miles suffered a sudden and fatal heart attack. Short of dying in the saddle perhaps, it was a most appropriate last exit for this man of immense and almost inexhaustible energy, the man who had performed some of the most remarkable feats of physical strength and skill in our military history.

The General's last appearance in the headlines was nationwide and impressive. Deskmen in newspaper city rooms who had never heard of Lieutenant General Nelson Appleton Miles dug into their morgues and came up with a long list of ancient distinctions dating back to the start of the Civil War. But very few of the long obituaries came even close to including all of the General's important accomplishments, and few gave any very clear idea of his exact status during the Spanish-American War—thanks again to the long-forgotten efforts of Roosevelt and Root, back in the days when they had tried to bury their most hated critic while he was still commanding general of the Army. President Coolidge attended the elaborate state funeral, at which all the highest military honors were accorded. Probably he hadn't the slightest idea he was in some part making amends for the absence of President Roosevelt at Miles' retirement reception so long ago.

Here I seem to have come to the end of my search. When it began, I was determined to be impartial. There would be many things about Miles, I was sure, which would not endear him to me. I thought of him as a crusty old relic of a period in our history that has never been any source of pride to me,

251

and a compatriot of some of my own ancestors I have not especially admired. It was his *importance* that first impressed me, not how *admirable* he might have been. I wanted to find out why in most encyclopedias Miles rated so much less space than Custer, whose chief distinction, while still young and a mere acting colonel, was to get himself and his men exterminated. Why so much less space than, say, Sheridan?

Here at the end, I must admit, I have become very much biased in favor of my subject. But it is only the old General himself who has won me over—his own books (terribly badly written as they are), his own life, his own personality, as the evidence has gradually unfolded. I see him now as a giant of an extinct breed, a man of such enormous strength and stubbornness that no amount of pressure could shape him to fit smoothly into the pattern of his time, a pattern made for lesser men.

A HISTORY OF WESTERN LITERATURE